Turning the Tide:
The Challenge Ahead

Report of the 2002
Scottish Church Census

D1334870

Turning the Tide: The Challenge Ahead

Report of the 2002
Scottish Church Census

Dr Peter Brierley

CHRISTIAN RESEARCH

The right of Peter Brierley to be identified as the author of this work has been
asserted by him in accordance with the Copyright, Designs and Patents Act 1988

First British edition May 2003

ISBN 1 85321 148 6 (CRA)

Published by Christian Research with the Church of Scotland
on behalf of the Scottish Church Census Steering Committee

Christian Research, Vision Building,
4 Footscray Road, Eltham, London SE9 2TZ
Tel: 020 8294 1989   Fax: 020 8294 0014
Email: admin@Christian-research.org.uk
Web: www.christian-research.org.uk

The Church of Scotland,
121 George Street, Edinburgh EH2 4YN
Tel: 0131-225 5722

British Library Cataloguing Data
A catalogue record for this book is available from the British Library.

No royalties are being paid for this book: any profit will be used
to strengthen church leadership in the days ahead.

Designed and produced for the publisher by:
Paul Jones Associates, 98 Eden Way, Beckenham, Kent BR3 3DH

Printed by Cox & Wyman, England

Contents

1) A pagan country?

The headline was very specific: "Scotland is pagan: it's official"[1]! The article went on to describe the findings of the Scottish Social Attitudes Survey, presented by Dr Steve Bruce, Professor of Sociology at the University of Aberdeen, to a conference held in May 2002. Certainly the figures made dismal reading.

Professor John Drane, School of Divinity and Religious Studies, also at Aberdeen University, in an indignant letter to the *Church of England Newspaper* protested that the *CEN* had misreported the survey. The survey, he said, "identified... that Scotland... is becoming more secular, with diminishing public interest in religious institutions.... The real challenge facing us is... the insidious secular materialism of our culture."[2]

Three weeks later another headline stated "Churches in Scotland dispute 'pagan' label"[3], and the subsequent article quoted the Primus of the Scottish Episcopal Church who argued "that to judge spirituality on the basis of church attendance was to miss the search for meaning by many people". That doubtless is true, but nevertheless to look in detail at church attendance can be useful. It may also help destroy the myth of a pagan Scotland!

Yes, another Census

The first Scottish Church Census which involved all the churches in Scotland was undertaken in 1984. Although the Steering Committee was under the chairmanship of the National Bible Society of Scotland (now the Scottish Bible Society), it contained representatives of all the major denominations in Scotland. The study followed similar work in England (in 1979) and in Wales (in 1982) and showed that 17% of Scottish people then attended Sunday worship[4].

A similar survey, but with more questions, followed 10 years later in 1994, again after a further English study (in 1989). The administrative arrangements were similar to 1984, and an excellent 81% response was achieved from the 4,000+ churches. This study showed that the percentage then attending Sunday worship in Scotland had fallen to 14%[5].

Following yet another English study (in 1998), the question was naturally raised again: should there be a further Scottish Church Census? In the interim, leadership had changed at the Scottish Bible Society, and the initiative this time came through the Board of National Mission in the Church of Scotland, whose General Secretary is Rev Douglas Nicol. A meeting held in Edinburgh early in 2001 was attended by representatives of all the main denominations and agreed that a further study would be very helpful.

A representative Steering Committee was formed, which met a number of times to monitor progress. It consisted of:
• Rev Colin Sinclair, Church of Scotland (Chair)
• Rev David Black, representing the Independent Churches
• Rev Ann Bradley, representing the Smaller Denominations
• Ronnie Convery, Roman Catholic Archdiocese of Glasgow
• Rev Canon Bob Fyffe, Scottish Episcopal Church
• Rev Douglas Hutcheon, Baptist Union of Scotland
• Rev Ann Inglis, Church of Scotland
• Peter Kearney, Catholic Media Office
• Gary Leach, Board of National Mission, Church of Scotland
• Rev Douglas Nicol, Board of National Mission, Church of Scotland

But why another Census? Behind any decision to embark on a major enterprise must lie important reasons. Some of these were examined at that 2001 meeting.

A Changing Scene

Many people have migrated to Scotland in the past decade, and while naturally this impacts the total population it also affects the balance of the population since many of these are people in their 30s or 40s. It can also influence the churchgoing population since the churchgoing habits of the immigrants may be quite different from Scottish people generally. Hence evaluating the age structure of Scottish churchgoers becomes especially important.

Several denominational changes have taken place in Scotland. The Baptist Union of Scotland for example is replacing its 15 associations with 9 regions, and the office of General Secretary is becoming a leadership team headed by a General Director[6]. Dr Jim Brooks of Queen's Park Baptist Church, Glasgow will be the final President. One of the smaller denominations, the Salvation Army in Scotland, is now part of the UK Territory. The Free Church of Scotland split into two groups in January 2000. The Scottish Congregational Church joined the United Reformed Church on 1st April 2000.

In addition, there have been huge political changes with the formation of the Scottish Parliament for the first time for nearly 300 years, with all the consequent administrative alteration that this both has and will still bring about. Some other administrative changes resulted from the amending of the boundaries of many Councils by the Boundary Commission. Consequently the previous area groupings by which church attendance was analysed need revision.

A Concerned Scene

Existing figures published regularly by the main denominations in Scotland show decreasing membership. The Church of Scotland membership for example decreased 10% in the last 5 years of the 20th century[7]. Most others did likewise. Attendance is also declining. Apart from the trends already observed from the 1984 and 1994 studies, numbers attending Mass in Roman Catholic churches in

Scotland, who conduct their own annual census, are dropping rapidly. It is important to know, however, how far this trend is similar to other denominations, and whether it is uniform across the whole of Scotland.

Of particular concern is the absence of young people from Sunday worship in Scotland. The English survey of 1998 showed a drastic drop in the numbers of children attending church, a loss of 1,000 a week overall[8], and it was a natural question to ask if the same trends were true in Scotland. Some research by the Church of Scotland had shown a preference by its young people to attend mid-week youth clubs rather than Sunday Bible Classes[9].

A third factor was less tangible but just as real: if change is needed (which many would accept is so), how best to change? What are the key parameters that need to be considered? Which are the priorities for the years immediately ahead? Could a survey help answer such vital questions?

A Comparative Scene

The English child attendance decline was of obvious concern to Scottish church leaders: was the same happening in Scotland? Young people are both today's church and tomorrow's church and trends here can be critical.

There is a huge evangelistic need. At the conference when he presented the "Scotland is pagan" findings, Professor Bruce said: "One of the main areas of concern must be that the vast majority of those who said they were not raised in a religious family have not been converted."[10] And perhaps not just those raised outside religious families! The Scottish Evangelism Survey reported "only a third of churches and ministries see evangelism as their single highest priority, yet the vast majority of church leaders believe that the members of their congregations should be more active in evangelism than they are now."[11]

There is also the interesting phenomenon of changing churchmanships. This emerged particularly in the 1998 English study which showed a marked growth in Mainstream Evangelicalism, but decline everywhere else. Could the same be true in Scotland? If so, why might that be, and what are its implications? The relevant question was asked in the 1994 Scottish Church Census, so could easily be repeated, and comparative data derived.

Why hold a census in 2002?

If the previous studies had been in 1984 and 1994 it would seem logical that the next Census should be in 2004. Why bring it forward? There were a number of reasons:

- It takes a long time to turn a big ship round. If the churches are to change in Scotland in a major way, the sooner that process can be begun the better.
- The rate of decline appears to be accelerating. Another benchmark thus becomes more useful more quickly.
- There were resources available at the time of the meeting (in 2001) to meet the costs. It isn't always certain that that state of affairs will continue!
- There was also a willingness to listen afresh to new evidence, and where necessary make changes. A subsequent survey[12] was to show that many Church of Scotland ministers suffer from stress; something of that pressure was already known in 2001, and with it the knowledge that some changes would have to be made.
- More and up-to-date information is required if strategic change is to be considered. In addition, extra information was required which had not been asked in earlier studies.
- Scottish society is rapidly changing, so taking the temperature now as it were seemed better than waiting (somewhat arbitrarily) a further two years.
- The "Scotland is pagan" headline had made the situation a burning issue just two weeks before the census took place.

There are no statistical problems inherent in asking for data at slightly different time intervals, so it was agreed that the next Scottish Church Census should go ahead in 2002. Subsequently the actual Sunday chosen was Sunday, 12th May 2002.

The value of a further Census

Trend information is important. Are things going up or down? They rarely stay the same. While the 1984 and 1994 Censuses had yielded useful information, another study near the beginning of the 21st century would show how church life had changed especially in the hectic years at the end of the old millennium. Thus another census could look at the emerging patterns of change with respect to gender and age (two key variables), denomination, churchmanship and geography.

The ethnic composition of a congregation had been included in the 1998 English survey, but it was decided not to include that question in Scotland. However the question on frequency of attendance which had been pioneered in the 1998 study was used in 2002, as were questions building on the findings in the English study of the importance of learning more about midweek activities.

As well as looking for growth and decline, it was felt important to also try to understand some of the reasons behind the findings. As a consequence, and for the first time in conjunction with a Church Census, some Focus Groups were simultaneously commissioned. These were held after the initial analysis had been completed, and thus were able to explore in depth a few of the preliminary results. Their findings have been integrated with this report at the salient places but are mainly to be found in Chapter 10.

With data spanning 18 years it is possible to attempt some longer term projections with a measure of confidence. Having an idea of where current trends will take you if they are not changed can be useful, both to help manage the positive trends and to think strategically about how to turn around the negative ones.

Leadership is crucial to the church just as it is to society and the nation. Providing as much strategic data as possible for leaders should therefore always be useful. This particular survey thus also asked some questions about local leadership, which hopefully will be helpful to national leadership in the different denominations.

Many of us love collecting photographs. They are useful reminders of where we've been, and importantly can help us recall key events and places we might otherwise have forgotten. A Church Census is a bit like taking a photograph of Scottish church life at a moment in time, so that, as well as giving a lot of information about that specific date, it also provides a general flavour which can be compared with earlier photographs.

Overall, the 2002 Census asked for a range of information not previously gathered across all of Scotland and thus will allow attention in planning for the future to focus on youth, fringe and midweek activities. The Census is a catalyst for information, which in an IT age becomes all the more useful.

How can the information be used?

There are a number of ways in which individual members of congregations or church leaders can use the information in this book and in the accompanying volume of *Religious Trends*[13]. The following suggestions may be helpful:
- Compare the changes in your own local church life with those of your denomination. Are they the same or different? If different, are yours better or worse? Aim to try and identify where your church is strong (so that you can build on those strengths) or weak (so that you can work to overcome those weaknesses).
- Similarly you can compare the results with your church's churchmanship, environment or geographical area. Again look for strengths and weaknesses.

- Especially compare the age and gender breakdown in your congregation with that shown for your denomination or geographical area. Where are you stronger? Weaker?
- Look at the places where the church is growing. What conclusions can you draw from that? How far can those conclusions be used to help you plan change in the coming year or two?
- There is much information here about leadership, midweek meetings and the importance of certain types of events. Can you apply this data to your own circumstances and form a strategic plan for how you wish to move forwards?
- You may wish to discuss this information with others, either in your local area or within your denomination. That's great! Thinking through things together is often helpful. One of the Proverbs observes that iron sharpens iron!
- Likewise we all need to pray for vision and clarity to think ahead. Pray for Scotland[14] (formerly the Scottish Prayer Centre) is already active, drawing charismatic and conservative streams together. How do we begin to reach effectively the many outside the church with the message of the Gospel? If Christianity is to make a difference to Scottish national life, more people need to become disciples of Jesus Christ. The National School of Evangelism[15] drew 500 people from 16 denominations to a conference entitled "Evangelism in the 3rd Millennium" in January 2003.
- Local planning also needs to take place in the context of central planning, at Synod, Presbytery or Headquarter level or wherever appropriate. Such planning is perhaps at the strategic level, but it needs to be broken down into operational level thinking where it can be put into action, thus allowing the tactical level to be successful[16].

How was the information collected?

The survey form was drawn up in association with the Steering Committee, sent to a small number of church leaders as a pilot exercise, and then finally printed and posted to each of the 4,144 church-es in Scotland in April 2002. We had written to them all in February to say it was coming, which also enabled us to check we had the correct addresses. There was also an early Press Release explaining the process, and all senior denominational leaders were informed of the study. We had a large number of encouraging letters back! A copy of the form is in the Appendix.

Some of the questions were difficult to get accurate answers for. So a pro forma was sent with the form which could be copied and used to give to each person attending services on 12th May, asking them to tick appropriately (and totally anonymously). These con-gregational responses were then collected and collated by the church before returning the Census form.

We are extremely grateful for the care and attention so many took with this procedure, and for the thousands that responded. Some took the trouble to write a detailed covering letter, and others made appropriate comments on the Census form. Some, finding their form had got lost in the post, were kind enough to complete another. Many took the trouble to phone with queries. A few churches used the exercise to analyse their own results in detail[17].

How good was the response?

We had a response rate of 52%, lower than in 1994, but higher than was achieved in England in 1998, and by normal marketing stan-dards in 2002 a very good response[18]. This was after sending a reminder, and asking senior leaders in all the larger denominations to encourage their clergy to respond. Statistically, the response is sufficient to give accurate results. There is always a small bias in any answer which is not based on a 100% response. In this case, an answer of 10% would be in the range of $\pm$ 1.3%, and an answer of 50% of $\pm$ 2.1%[19].

Broken down by denomination, the response was:

- 64% from the Church of Scotland (out of 1,666 churches)
- 63% from the Episcopal churches (out of 309 churches)
- 54% from the Baptist churches (out of 204 churches)
- 43% from the Other Presbyterian churches (out of 342 churches)
- 43% from the Roman Catholic churches (out of 594 churches)
- 43% collectively from the various Smaller Denominations (out of 470 churches), and
- 28% from the Independent churches (out of 559 churches).

Estimated attendances were applied to the churches which did not reply, which were initially simply pro rata to those in the same denomination. The collective results were however then tested against existing trends and known data where that was available.

In this process in evaluating the Roman Catholic data, which collects Mass attendance figures every year, we discovered to our horror that the 1994 results had counted the Catholic children twice, once in the category "children" (correctly) and again in the category "adults" (incorrectly). We have therefore had to revise the 1994 Catholic figures throughout, and took the opportunity to align the Catholic figures not to our estimates from the previous Censuses, but to their actual numbers.

We have not separated children and adults in the 2002 results, although the breakdown is readily available through the age analysis. We have simply used total Sunday church attendance figures, which excludes those who attended more than once. The figures are therefore of attenders, and not of attendances. They may therefore be compared with population figures.

How is the data analysed?

All forms were computerised, but the data is held totally confidentially. The results from any individual congregation are not released to anyone, even serious researchers, without prior permission in writing from the church concerned. There are four broad control variables which are applied to all the data, and which when totalled together by any of these four paths give the same overall total figures. These are denomination, churchmanship, environment and geographical area.

There were 49 different *denominations* in Scotland in 2002, some very small, and others large. The Church of Scotland and the Roman Catholic Church between them accounted for three-quarters, 75%, of all churchgoers, so the remaining denominations together make up the other 25%. For simplicity of analysis, these are put into seven groupings[20]:

- The Church of Scotland
- The Other Presbyterian churches (including the Free Church of Scotland, the Continuing Free Church, the United Free Church, the Reformed Presbyterian, the Free Presbyterian and Associated Presbyterian churches)
- The Episcopal Church of Scotland
- The Baptist churches (Baptist Union, Grace Baptist and Independent Baptists)
- The Independent Churches (the New or House Churches and their various streams, the Christian Brethren, Congregational churches, FIEC, Churches of Christ, and churches for overseas nationals or immigrants)
- The Smaller Denominations (Methodists, Salvation Army, Lutheran, Orthodox, Nazarenes, Pentecostal denominations, Quakers, Local Ecumenical Projects (LEPs), United Reformed, Seventh-Day Adventist, Worldwide Church of God, and Military chaplaincies)
- The Roman Catholic Church (including a few immigrant Catholic churches).

The *churchmanships* were derived from nine specific items on the form, the minister being invited to tick up to three to describe his/her congregation. These combinations are then used to derive six groups: Broad, Catholic, Evangelical, Liberal, Low Church and Reformed. The Evangelical category is further broken down into:

Reformed, Mainstream and Charismatic Evangelicals.

The *environment* of each church was not asked again in 2002 as the 1994 answers to this question were considered adequate. There are eight categories: City Centre, Urban Priority Area, Housing Scheme, Suburban, Town, New Town, Dormitory Rural Area and Other Rural Areas[21].

Scotland is divided up by *geographical area* into 32 Councils. The 1984 Census was analysed by 21 area units, mostly counties, and the 1994 into 24 units. These have all been reworked in the light of the changes made by the Boundary Commission, some of which required very extensive and detailed work[22], and the results have been analysed into 26 areas. These have followed the earlier studies as much as possible, but are completely contiguous with the borders of the 32 Councils. The one exception of the Districts of Skye and Lochalsh have been left with the Western Isles as in previous studies, and are therefore not part of Highland. In this process details of some Councils have been added together; these are:

• North, East and South Ayrshire are taken together as "Ayrshire"
• Renfrewshire and East Renfrewshire
• Mid and East Lothian
• Stirling and Clackmannanshire
• Highland and Argyll & Bute.

So what does all this mean?

Scottish church leaders in 2001 felt that a further Scottish Church Census would be a valuable resource for Scottish churches. They consequently commissioned Christian Research in London to undertake it, the same body that had undertaken the previous studies. The 2002 Scottish Church Census received a statistically viable response level, and the results have been analysed by four broad criteria: denomination, churchmanship, environment and geographical area.

NOTES

[1] Article in the *Church of England Newspaper,* London, 2nd May 2002, Page 4.

[2] Letter to the *Church of England Newspaper,* London, 30th May 2002, Page 17.

[3] Article by Pat Ashworth in the *Church Times,* 24th May 2002.

[4] *Prospects for Scotland,* Peter Brierley and Fergus MacDonald, MARC Europe, London and National Bible Society of Scotland, Edinburgh, 1985, Page 60.

[5] *Prospects for Scotland 2000,* Peter Brierley and Fergus MacDonald, Christian Research, London and National Bible Society of Scotland, Edinburgh, 1995, Page 112.

[6] Report "Sweeping changes north of the border", *Baptist Times,* 7th November 2002, Page 3.

[7] Figures are available in *Religious Trends,* No 3, 2002/2003, Christian Research, London, 2001, Table 8.7.2.

[8] *The Tide is Running Out,* Peter Brierley, Christian Research, London, 2000, Table 27, Page 97.

[9] *Church of Scotland: Ministry among Young People,* research report by Christian Research, 2001 for Parish Education Department, Church of Scotland.

[10] Op cit (Footnote 1).

[11] The Scotland Evangelism Survey was undertaken by the Billy Graham Evangelistic Association in preparation for the January 2003 National School of Evangelism. Reported in *Christian Herald,* 26th October 2002.

[12] Undertaken in 2002 by *Life and Work,* the magazine of the Church of Scotland, which found "more than a quarter of clergy struggling in their marriages because of the demands of their post" as an article in the *CEN* of 10th October 2002 put it.

[13] *Religious Trends,* No 4, 2003/2004, edited by Peter Brierley. Published in June 2003 at £20 (postage extra), it gives very extensive coverage by geographical area as well as many coloured maps by denomination or churchmanship. It is available from all good bookshops or direct from Christian Research, Vision Building, 4 Footscray Road, Eltham, London SE9 2TZ, or phone 020 8294 1989, or fax 020 8294 0014, or visit our website www.christian-research.org.uk.

[14] Details available from PO Box 8987, Lanark ML11 9AR, or look at their website www.prayforscotland.com

[15] Details from Mission Scotland, 9 Canal Street, Glasgow G4 0AB, or look at their website www.missionscotland.com

[16] More information on this terminology can be found in the forthcoming book *Coming up Trumps: building vision, thinking strategically and playing to win,* to be published by Christian Research, London, in 2003.

[17] Such as Deeside Christian Fellowship Church, which produced a careful 8 page analysis.

[18] Unfortunately some mail went missing in the post. Most Congregational churches never received their original form, and were sent another some weeks later when one of their ministers queried why they had been left out of the Census. At least one bundle of responses from the Scottish Borders never arrived and we had to write to all those churches again. We reckon perhaps the response rate would have been 2% higher if these mishaps had not occurred.

[19] Using the normal 95% confidence level.

[20] A full list is given in the Methodology section on Page 12.2 of *Religious Trends,* No 4. See Footnote 13.

[21] We do not use the Office of National Statistics classification (as given in *Population Trends* Number 102, Winter 2000, Page 20) because, of the 14 categories they specify, only 5 are used to describe Scotland: Education Centres (Aberdeen and Edinburgh), Industrial areas (the large majority of the middle urban belt stretching from Glasgow to Fife), Mixed Urban areas (Stirling, East Renfrewshire and East Lothian), New and Developing Areas (Mid and West Lothian only), with the whole of the rest of Scotland classified as Remoter Rural.

[22] For example, 19 churches on the west of old Dunbartonshire were located in an area which was moved into Argyll and Bute. We had to know the denomination, church-manship, environment and size of those churches to transfer them out of one Council into another in order to make trend comparisons!

2) Churchgoing trends since 1984

The angelic instruction in Revelation 11 is "Count those who are worshipping". The Scottish Church Census did not use the measuring rod described in that chapter, but it did seek to count the number of people attending church on 12th May 2002.

On that Sunday, there were 570,130 people in church across Scotland, some of whom attended more than once, 11.2% of the country's population[1]. The total figure represents an 18% decline over the eight years since 1994 when 691,120 people attended church. That in turn was a 19% drop on the 1984 figure of 853,700. Since the 18% drop was over 8 years (an average annual decline of –2.4%) and the 19% over 10 years (an average annual rate of –2.1%) it is unfortunately true that the rate of decline of church attendance in Scotland is accelerating. The same is also true in England.

These figures represent a large body of people who are attending church, and are almost certainly larger than for any other voluntary institution in Scotland. For example, they are more than double the total average weekly attendance at Scottish football league matches (4.5% of the population)[2].

Change by denomination

Although there were nearly 50 denominations in Scotland in 2002, the two largest, the Church of Scotland and the Roman Catholic Church accounted for 75% of the total church attendance. In 1984, however, they accounted for 83% of the total, showing that these two major denominations have declined faster than the many smaller ones. Table 2.1 gives the basic figures:

Table 2.1: Churchgoers by denomination, 1984–2002

Denomination	1984	% change	1994	% change	2002	% of total 2002
Church of Scotland	361,340	*–19*	293,170	*–22*	228,500	**40**
Roman Catholic	345,950	*–28*	249,720	*–19*	202,110	**35**
Independent	39,370	*+22*	48,020	*–6*	45,010	**8**
Smaller denominations	29,120	*+5*	30,500	*–11*	28,640	**5**
Baptist	29,240	*–16*	24,530	*+1*	24,830	**5**
Other Presbyterian	28,680	*–19*	23,310	*–5*	22,170	**4**
Episcopal	20,000	*+2*	20,350	*–7*	18,870	**3**
Total All Scotland	**853,700**	*–19*	**691,120**	*–18*	**570,130**	**100**

In the 1984 to 1994 period the Independent, Smaller Denominations and the Episcopal Church all grew, but in the period 1994 to 2002 all three of these declined, while the Baptists recorded a slender growth. As it happens, the same was true of the Baptists in England between 1989 and 1998. The Table shows the greater declines of the two largest churches against the lesser proportionate changes in the smaller ones. Table 2.1 looks at the denominational groups; as we shall see, some of the individual denominations within those groups grew, not declined.

In previous studies figures for church attendance were also collected for 1980 and 1990. As the period between these years and 1984 and 1994 varies from four to six years comparisons over time can be awkward. Figure 2.2 shows the figures calculated at five year intervals which makes it easier to see that the declines that have taken place in the two major denominations have not been replicated to anything like the same extent collectively amongst the smaller denominations.

If present trends continue to 2005, then total Sunday church attendance will be only 10.1% of the population by then, a further drop of 10% in numbers over the three years 2002 to 2005. The decrease becomes faster because older people have much higher mortality rates.

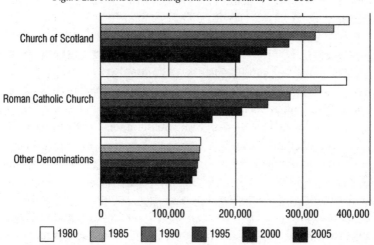

Figure 2.2: Numbers attending church in Scotland, 1980–2005

□ 1980   ▨ 1985   ▨ 1990   ■ 1995   ■ 2000   ■ 2005

In the last eight years Scottish churches have seen attendance decline by a net 120,990 people, or 15,120 a year, which is almost 300 people a week. As the average congregation is 140 people this, in effect, is like losing two churches every single week, twice the rate of 1994. Churches are not actually closing at this rate; congregations are simply getting smaller. There were 4,164 churches in Scotland in 1994; eight years later there were 4,144, just 20 fewer.

Having so many churches represents a huge opportunity for service and outreach.

Growth and decline

It would be wrong to picture this decline as universal. The figure is a net figure, that is, it is the difference between gains and losses. Some churches are growing while others are declining. Those in the latter category outweigh those in the former. So the question becomes, why do people join a church and why do they leave? These are important questions, and answers will come as different analyses are made of the figures.

It is worth noting, however, that the population of Scotland, as in other parts of the UK, is more mobile than it used to be, often moving for employment reasons. Such movement is bound to include churchgoers, and for many churches a major reason of change is that people move out and thus leave, while newcomers are likely to be people who move into the parish or "catchment area" of their church rather than outsiders being "won". People are also more willing to transfer from one church to another without necessarily moving house.

The decline in church attendance, however, was not primarily due to population change. Over the 18 years 1984 to 2002 the Scottish population declined 2%; by comparison the number of people in church on Sunday dropped 33%.

We look at the age of churchgoers later, but with almost a third (31%) of Scotland's churchgoers 65 or over, "being promoted to glory" (as the Salvation Army describes it) will also be a major factor in the declining numbers of some congregations.

While mobility and death cause congregational change, what are some of the reasons for growth? Research in England has identified some of the marks of churches which are larger and/or growing. The Focus Groups found these applied in Scotland also (see Chapter 10). They are:

• A clear vision of what the church wants to do
• A senior leader with the gift of leadership (which comes in many varying forms!)
• Relevant preaching ("explains what the Bible means")
• High quality worship
• Friendly people who give a warm welcome
• The presence of people of all ages (and life-stages)
• The opportunity to "belong" to a family if desired
• A good range of activities for all ages, especially for children and young people.

People seem to come initially to church primarily because they want fellowship, a spiritual home, and know of the church's reputation (usually through a friend). They stay primarily because of the preaching, the worship, an easy-to-follow service, the welcome, the range of activities, and the personality of the leader.

The minister is crucial. His/her *personality* effectively directs the culture of the church. His *gifting* is the attraction behind the teaching. His *motivations* – achieving and affiliating – drive the church. People rarely come to his church because of *who he is* (or his life-stage) since the church is large enough to cater for all; they come because of what he *does* (interpret scripture meaningfully). He/she needs to be: a good communicator, a team leader, with a vision and some administrative ability.

Groups of denominations

The census necessarily had to group some of the smaller denominations for analysis. But those in these denominations naturally wish to know how they have fared if only in the macro measurement of total attendance. There are three groups, and details of their individual denominations follow in the order they were given in Table 2.1. Figures broken down by the individual churches are only available for 1990 not 1984.

1) The Independent denominations

A breakdown of the main groups within this broad category is given in Table 2.3 overleaf.

The Christian Brethren have seen modest growth; in total over 300 congregations are represented. Their collective growth is primarily because there are a small number of Open Brethren churches which are quite large and growing.

The New or House Churches have not fared so well in the eight years 1994 to 2002, in contrast to their earlier growth. But that growth reflected the movement as a whole across England, and the

Table 2.3: Sunday attendance for the independent denominations, 1990–2002

Denomination	1990	% change	1994	% change	2002
Christian Brethren	18,880	−9	17,090	+6	18,200
New Churches	9,770	+47	14,340	−16	12,020
Congregational Churches	11,090	0	11,130	−23	8,580
Other Churches	4,740	+15	5,460	+14	6,210
Total Independent Churches	**44,400**	**+8**	**48,020**	**−6**	**45,010**

decline in recent years also tallies with their experience in the north of England where decline rather than growth (which continues in the south) has been the norm.

The Congregational Churches collectively have declined at about the same rate as the major denominations in Scotland in the past eight years. This is partly because many (but not all) of their congregations have relatively large numbers of elderly people.

The Other Churches group has continued to grow as it did between 1984 and 1994, but at a slower rate. This group includes the Church of the Nazarene which has doubled its ministerial strength in Scotland in the last 20 years, and continues to see modest growth, presumably because of this leadership. This group also includes the Fellowship of Independent Evangelical Churches (FIEC) which again has seen modest growth. The largest churches in this broad Other Churches group are those which are totally independent, congregations which stand alone, few in number but generally thriving, giving again a linkage between size and growth.

2) The Smaller Denominations

The other denominations, often part of much larger international networks, are given in more detail in Table 2.4, overleaf.

The Smaller Denominations group is made up of two contrasting sections. The Salvation Army have grown slightly, perhaps helped by their changed administrative structure. Nearly half of the Pentecostal churches are Elim, a fifth are Assemblies of God,

Table 2.4: Sunday attendance for the smaller denominations, 1990–2002

Denomination	1990	% change	1994	% change	2002
Pentecostal Churches	6,710	+36	9,120	+11	10,090
Salvation Army	7,270	−10	6,510	+8	7,040
Methodists	7,320	−18	6,000	−33	4,040
Other Denominations	7,780	−2	7,650	−33	5,120
Local Ecumenical Churches	1,420	+93	2,740	−14	2,350
Total Smaller Denominations	**30,500**	**+5**	**32,020**	**−11**	**28,640**

a further fifth the smaller, and often black-led, Pentecostal groups, and the remaining tenth belong to the Apostolic Church. These Pentecostal groups also grew (unlike their English counterparts) overall, but this was spearheaded by the independent and ethnic congregations.

The Methodists and the other smaller groups declined. Amongst the latter are the Religious Society of Friends, the United Reformed Church, and the Seventh-Day Adventists. All these have relatively high proportions of older people, who drop out of regular attendance because of health or transport difficulties, because they go into care, or because of death. The Orthodox churches are also among these smaller congregations, and, as in England, these grew – in Scotland modestly, in England greatly. In the postmodern 21st century something in Orthodox spirituality appeals!

There are a few more Local Ecumenical Projects in Scotland now than in 1994, but, notwithstanding, their congregations collectively are smaller. Their growth in the early 1990s was mainly due to a doubling of the number of LEPs.

3) Other Presbyterian Churches

The smaller Presbyterian denominations are given instead in Table 2.5 overleaf. They collectively have not decreased as much as the main Presbyterian body, the Church of Scotland. This is particularly because of the growth in attendance amongst the smallest of these

Table 2.5: Sunday attendance for other Presbyterian denominations, 1990–2002

Denomination	1990	% change	1994	% change	2002
Free Church of Scotland (A) ⎫	17,260	–10	15,510	–8	12,810
Free Church of Scotland (B) ⎭					1,520
United Free Church of Scotland	6,560	–11	5,840	–8	5,370
Other Presbyterian Churches	2,180	–10	1,960	+26	2,470
Total Smaller Denominations	**28,680**	**–19**	**23,310**	**–5**	**22,170**

(A) Free Church of Scotland (B) Free Church of Scotland (Continuing)

denominations: the Reformed Presbyterian Church of Scotland has seen modest growth amongst its four congregations, as has the Free Presbyterian Church of Scotland. The Associated Presbyterian Churches, a group which began in 1989 with 33 congregations, has also seen growth.

Is it perhaps the less institutional churches in this group which have grown? While the others in this group have declined, they have declined at about the same rate as the other smaller denominations in Scotland, apart from the Baptists.

Number of churches and average congregational size

Table 2.6 gives the number of churches in 1994 and 2002 and the average congregational size[3]. "Churches" includes all ecclesiastical buildings used for worship, but also includes congregations meeting in homes, schools or other public places for worship. Military and school chapels are included where relevant, and convent and hospital services if open to the public.

The change in the number of churches is not at all correlated to the change in attendance. The Catholics have much larger congregations than other denominations; the figure in brackets in the Total line is the average size of churches if the Catholics were excluded. The Table shows that the Baptists which were about average size in 1994 are above average size in 2002; they are the only group whose average size has increased (although the Independents, Other Presbyterians and Episcopal congregations have barely changed).

Table 2.6: Number of churches and average congregations, 1994 and 2002

| | Number of churches | | | Average size | |
Denomination	1994	% change	2002	1994	2002
Church of Scotland	1,691	−1.5	1,666	173	137
Roman Catholic	598	−0.7	594	418	340
Independent	577	−3.1	559	83	81
Smaller denominations	432	+8.8	470	74	61
Baptist	203	+0.5	204	121	122
Other Presbyterian	352	−2.8	342	66	65
Episcopal	311	−0.6	309	65	61
Total	**4,164**	**−0.5**	**4,144**	**166**	**138**
All Scotland				**(124)**	**(104)**

The next Table shows the size of congregations in Scotland. Again the figures in brackets in the total line are the average for churches excluding the Catholics because the sizes of their churches are so different.

A third, 30%, of the churches in Scotland have 50 or fewer people present on a Sunday, just over a fifth, 22%, have between 51 and 100 people, slightly more, 26%, have between 101 and 200, and a fifth, 22%, including a large number of Catholic congregations, have more than 200.

Half of Scotland's Protestant churchgoers go to just 15% of Scotland's churches, as shown in Figure 2.8, a percentage the same as in England in 1998, and which compares with 18% in the United States in 1996.

Table 2.7: Percentages of churches by size and denomination, 2002

					Size of congregation					
Denomination	<10 %	11 –25 %	26 –50 %	51 –100 %	101 –150 %	151 –200 %	201 –300 %	301 –400 %	>400 %	Avge size
Church of Scotland	1	5	12	17	26	13	17	5	4	137
Roman Catholic	0	5	6	14	11	8	13	10	33	340
Independent	2	15	21	34	11	7	5	3	2	81
Smaller denoms.	11	16	23	28	10	5	6	1	0	61
Baptist	1	7	13	28	21	12	9	4	5	122
Other Presbyterian	12	19	25	23	8	7	2	2	2	65
Episcopal	10	14	25	30	10	6	4	0	1	61
All Scotland	*4*	*10*	*16*	*22*	*17*	*9*	*11*	*4*	*7*	*138*
Overall Protestants	*(4)*	*(10)*	*(17)*	*(24)*	*(18)*	*(10)*	*(11)*	*(3)*	*(3)*	*(104)*

Figure 2.8: Protestant churchgoers and churches

People   Churches

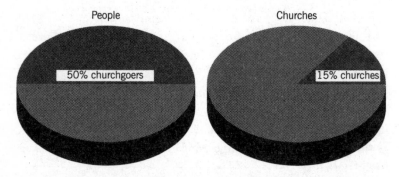

50% churchgoers   15% churches

The average size of the congregation attended by the 50% in the 15% largest churches is 270, three times the average size (90) attended by the other 50% in the majority (85%) of smaller churches. The experience of half Scotland's churchgoers is therefore of large churches, usually where there are many capable people to help do all the work. Is this why so many people go to such churches? As mentioned above, the answer is partly YES, because larger churches usually have the resources of people, finances and programme to enable a breadth of regular activities to take place and can provide quality worship. Perhaps they employ a Youth Worker as well.

One Catholic church in 14, 7%, sees more than a thousand people at Mass every Sunday, and 1% more than 2,000. Half of Catholic churchgoers go to 16% of their churches, the average size of which is 1,060 people. The other half go to 84% of their churches whose average size is 200, a fifth of the others.

Growth and decline

Another question in the 2002 Census not asked previously in Scotland was "By 2010 do you expect your church to have..." and five options were given relating to growth and decline. Table 2.9 shows how different denominations answered the question, and Figure 2.10 illustrates the overall results.

Table 2.9: Anticipated growth and decline by 2010 by denomination

Denomination	Grown significantly %	Grown a little %	Remained stable %	Declined %	Closed %
Church of Scotland	12	39	25	22	2
Roman Catholic	7	39	28	25	1
Independent	40	30	14	14	2
Smaller denominations	32	34	17	15	2
Baptist	48	38	8	6	0
Other Presbyterian	16	37	20	21	6
Episcopal	17	47	23	12	1
Total All Scotland	20	37	22	19	2

Figure 2.10: Anticipated growth and decline by 2010 for all Scottish churches

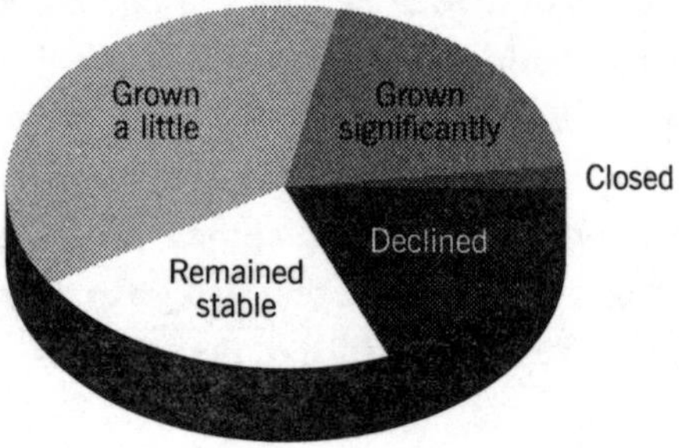

Nearly three-fifths, 57%, of the churches in Scotland expect to grow in the eight years 2002 to 2010, and a third of these to grow "significantly" (a word which the questionnaire did not define). This represents a considerable body of optimism for the future. Just over a fifth, 22%, expect to remain stable or static, and a further fifth, 19%, expect to decline.

While only 2% expect to actually close, that is still equivalent to 83 churches, four times the net change that has actually taken place over the last 8 years. No Baptist churches expect to close (which is consistent with the denomination actually growing), but 6% of "Other Presbyterian" churches expect to close, about a quarter of the overall total. Where would the churches close? 9% of those in Dumfries and Galloway expected to close by 2010, and 5% of the churches in Falkirk.

Where did the churches expect to grow[4]? Over three-quarters, 78%, said they would have grown by 2010 in Eilean Siar (the Western Isles, here including the Isle of Skye and Lochalsh), while 72% were expecting to grow in East and Mid Lothian and 71% in East Dunbartonshire. Growth is expected in quite different parts of Scotland – which is good! The smallest percentage, 21%, was in the Orkney Islands.

Those expecting to grow vary by denomination also, with at least half of the churches of all denominations except the Catholics expecting to do so. If that expectation can become reality, the situation could become very different in the years ahead. The Catholics, Church of Scotland and Episcopal are those most anticipating remaining stable, and the first two, along with the Other Presbyterians, have the most who expect to see decline.

Age and gender

The proportion of men in church in Scotland continues to increase! From 37% in 1984, it grew to 39% in 1994 and in 2002 stands at 40%. This is, however, rather due to women leaving than more men coming, a feature explored in a later chapter.

Age is also explored in more detail later, but the Table below shows the change in numbers attending by decadal age-group since 1984. Here the 8 year gap between 1994 and 2002 instead of 10 years makes the comparison less exact, but the general trend is very clear. Thus, for example, of the 142,000 children aged 0 to 9 attending church in 1984, by 1994 (when they were aged 10 to 19) only 76,000 were attending church (a 53% drop), and by 2002 (when most were

Table 2.11: Numbers attending by age-group, 1984–2002

Age-group	1984	1994	2002	% change 84–02	% change 94–02
0–9 years	142,280	82,940	65,610		
10–19 years	113,830	76,020	56,610		−32
20–29 years	76,840	55,290	36,710	−74	−52
30–39 years	85,370	78,330	53,880	−53	−3
40–49 years	93,910	85,810	66,100	−14	−16
50–59 years	102,440	93,300	78,320	−8	−9
60–69 years	109,820	98,480	91,280	−3	−2
70–79 years	85,930	79,480	79,920	−22	−19
80 years and over	43,280	41,470	41,700	−62	−48
Total attendance	**853,700**	**691,120**	**570,130**	**−33**	**−18**

aged 20 to 29) only 37,000 were attending church, a further drop of 52% since 1994 and a total drop out of 74% over the full 18 years. No church can survive that kind of exit rate!

The final columns give the equivalent of the 52% and 74% for each age cohort. The drop out rate becomes much less [in the "84–02" column] for those who were in their 30s and 40s in 1984 (that is, were born 1934 to 1953). The rate increases then simply because of normal mortality. The generation born before, during or immediately after World War II therefore have tended to stay in church; later generations have tended to leave. This pattern has been observed before in England and reflects the changing culture in the UK, and the oft-mentioned "generation gap".

The final column in Table 2.11 shows the large number of those aged 10 to 19 in 1994 who have left the church in the eight years since. This is a feature of English church life as well, but a more detailed survey of the age-group[5] has shown that it is 12 to 14 year olds who have left, whereas in Scotland it has tended to be those aged 15 to 19.

The worry in these figures is that the previous 1994 survey also showed a huge decline in the number of teenagers attending church in Scotland. It would appear that efforts to stem that tide, Canute-like, have been unsuccessful. What means should now be tried to encourage young people to stay in the church? Why do those who leave do so?

Frequency of attendance

The 2002 Census asked respondents to give the frequency with which members of their congregation attended. Not all gave this information, although a means of collecting it was provided. Half, 51%, of churches obtained the frequency directly from respondents, the other half, 49%, estimated them, but there was no statistical difference between actual and estimated figures (which occurred also in the English survey). Replies are summarised in Table 2.12.

Comparable information from earlier years is not available

except for the percentage who attended church twice weekly. In 1984 it was 13%, in 1994 14%, and in 2002 12%. That the "twicer" percentage has remained virtually constant over 18 years says something for the commitment and tenacity in a significant number of Scottish churchgoers.

Some churches, especially those in rural areas, only hold one service on a Sunday, so attending twice would be rather difficult! This may partly explain the low figure in the first column for the Church of Scotland and the Episcopal Churches. It is clear, however,

Table 2.12: Frequency of attending church, by denomination, 2002

Denomination	Twice weekly %	Weekly %	Fortnightly %	Monthly %	Quarterly %	Once or twice a year %	Visitors %
Church of Scotland	4	43	9	7	9	25	3
Roman Catholic	5	68	5	4	1	15	2
Independent	26	46	5	3	6	11	3
Smaller denominations	18	41	6	6	5	21	3
Baptist	25	45	5	6	4	12	3
Other Presbyterian	35	42	7	6	3	5	2
Episcopal	2	30	12	7	5	26	18
Total All Scotland	12	46	7	6	6	19	4

that the smaller denominations generally not only hold two services on a Sunday but expect many of their flock to attend!

The overall figures show that 58% of Scottish churchgoers attend every week. As churchgoers are 11.2% of the population, that means that 6.5% of the entire population regularly goes to church every week in Scotland, a figure half as big again as in England (where it is 4.4%), and half as many as attend football (who may not attend every week)! However, in addition to these weekly regulars others come at varying intervals.

On any given Sunday, of the total Scottish population:

- 6.5% will be in church because they go every week
- 4.7% more will be in church that week, though they go less regularly
  Thus,
- 11.2% attend church in any one week
- 14.3% attend church in any month
- 15.5% attend church in the course of a quarter, and
- 19.4% attend church at least once a year.

Scotland has half as many people again proportionately attending church on a weekly basis as does England (11.2% to 7.5%), but about the same proportions who attend less regularly. This suggests that the "occasionals" are much the same north and south of the border (and perhaps are occasional for similar reasons), but in Scotland there are more who are committed to weekly churchgoing, and it is in this commitment that the Scots differ from the English. This is an important strength.

The percentage who are visitors in any particular week in Scotland is much the same as in England, except for the Episcopal Church of Scotland. Why they should have so many visitors is unclear!

Other questions

Growth and decline were measured for other characteristics, like churchmanship and the environment, but these results are given in Chapter 5. Figures for the questions not looked at in this chapter – finance (Chapter 3), midweek meetings (Chapter 7) and leadership (Chapter 9) are given in the chapter indicated.

So what does this overview over time say?

This chapter has shown:

- A large number of people attend church in Scotland, with 570,000 present on an average week, more than twice the proportion of the population who attend football league matches (11.2% to 4.5%). Such a number is significant for any voluntary institution.
- The number of people attending church in Scotland had dropped by 18% in 2002, measured from 1994. This is a slightly faster rate of decline than the 19% experienced over the previous 10 years from 1984.
- The decrease was not primarily due to population change, as the Scottish population had only decreased 2% between 1984 and 2002.
- The Baptists grew in the period 1994 to 2002, the only major denomination to do so, although only by 1%. Some of the small denominations also grew. The denominations which declined most were the Church of Scotland (a fall of 22%) and the Roman Catholics (a fall of 19%).
- The smaller Presbyterian denominations collectively have seen growth in the eight years since 1994. So have the smaller Independent denominations, and the Christian Brethren. Amongst the "Smaller Denominations" group, the Salvation Army, Pentecostals and Orthodox have also seen modest growth in the same period.
- Congregations are getting smaller, rather than churches closing in line with declining numbers. There is still much residual strength in the number of churches, 4,144 across Scotland.
- The average Protestant Sunday congregation in 2002 was 104, Catholics 340. In 1994 the figures were 124 and 418 respectively.
- Other research has shown that clear vision, good leadership and relevant preaching are hallmarks of growing churches.
- A third, 30%, of Scottish churches have 50 or fewer people present on a Sunday. Just over a fifth, 22%, have between 51 and 100 people, and slightly more, 26%, have between 101 and 200. A fifth, 22%, including a large number of Catholic congregations, have more than 200.
- 50% of Scottish churchgoers attend 15% of churches.

- One person in 8, that is, 12%, who attends church goes twice on a Sunday, a percentage practically unaltered over 18 years. This shows a stronger commitment than exists for example in England.
- While large numbers of young people (under 30) have dropped out of church in the last 20 years in Scotland, as they have in England and other Western countries also, this is much less for those under 15 in Scotland than in England in the most recent eight year period. It is those who are now in their 60s who have dropped out least; numbers of those in their 70s or over have declined, but mainly because of death.
- Three-fifths, 58%, of Scottish churchgoers attend church at least once every week, equivalent to 6.5% of the entire population.
- Three-fifths, 57%, of congregations are expecting to grow by 2010. The percentage is much higher amongst Independent (70%) and Baptist (86%) churches. Conversely a fifth, 19%, of congregations expect to decline, and 2% to close altogether (6% of Other Presbyterians). Such expectations should give some cause for hope for the future.
- Growth by 2010 is expected most in Eilean Siar (the Western Isles, here including the Isle of Skye and Lochalsh) (78%), East and Mid Lothian (72%) and East Dunbartonshire (71%).

Growth (and decline) are clearly critical factors, and are not uniform across Scotland, either by denomination, age, leadership expectation or geographical area. It may readily be argued that growing congregations are just a mathematical element of church life (albeit an important element), but it is not the only element, and other concerns (such as spiritual well-being) are equally important and must be taken into consideration. While that is very true, the sheer scale of the decline has to be of major concern as the implications are so momentous.

It is equally true, however, that in some of these figures are signs of hope – the commitment of the 12% who attend church twice every week, the high percentage who expect their congregation to grow, a similar number of centres of worship as eight years ago, a good number of strong congregations, and still a large number of people involved in total – over 11% of the population is high by comparison with many European countries.

NOTES

[1] Throughout we have used the revised population figures issued by the Registrar General for Scotland in respect of the 2001 Population Census. Actual figures are published in *2001 Population Report Scotland,* General Register Office for Scotland, Edinburgh, September 2002.

[2] Taken from the Scottish Football website 4th February 2003.

[3] 1984 figures are given in *Religious Trends,* No 4, 2003/2004, Christian Research, Table 12.3.2.

[4] The figures in this paragraph are taken from Figure 3 on respective pages in Section 12 of *Religious Trends,* No 4, 2003/2004, Christian Research, London, 2003.

[5] *Reaching and Keeping Tweenagers,* Peter Brierley, Christian Research, London, January 2003.

3) Geographical variations in attendance

The Scottish Boundary Commission made sweeping changes to the boundaries of Scottish Councils, which necessitated the re-working of many of the results of the 1984 and 1994 Scottish Church Censuses. Details of churchgoing broken down by denomination, churchmanship, environment and age/gender are given in *Religious Trends* No 4, 2003/2004 for each of 26 areas (into which Scotland's 32 Councils have been combined)[1]. This chapter looks at the geographical variations by denomination; most other factors are considered geographically in the chapter discussing the appropriate topic.

Church attendance in 2002 by geographical area

Table 3.1 gives the basic information on Sunday attendance by the 26 Councils or areas used in this study. It is ordered into four groups as given by the percentage of the population attending church in 2002 (the figures in bold in the centre of the Table), with the highest first.

The first group of five areas (6 Councils) are those where the percentage attending church, 17% of the population, is well above the average for Scotland as as whole, 11.2%. These are all Councils west of a line drawn North West – South East through Clackmannanshire. They are all areas where the Roman Catholic Church is strong (over 50% of all attenders) except the Western Isles (Eilean Siar) with Skye and Lochalsh where the Free Church of Scotland dominates (also with over 50%). Consequently in all these areas the Church of Scotland is less well represented, with between a quarter and third of all churchgoers. These Councils have seen numbers drop, however, and at about the average rate for the whole country. But attendance there is high because of either the Free Kirk or Catholic strength.

The second group consists of six areas (9 Councils) where church attendance is above average, but not conspicuously so. Overall it is 12%. Apart from East Dunbartonshire, they have seen slightly smaller declines in church attendance overall – 16% (excluding East Dunbartonshire) against 18% altogether. Again, apart from the Orkney and Shetland Islands, these areas are all west of the vertical line through Clackmannanshire. The denominational spread is uneven – there are few Catholics on the Northern Isles; Highland is strong with Other Presbyterians; over half of churchgoers in Ayrshire are Church of Scotland.

The third group consists of nine areas (10 Councils) where church attendance is slightly lower than the national average at 10%. The average decline in numbers was 20%, slightly higher than the 18% nationally. More attend the Church of Scotland in these areas than across Scotland as whole (47% to 40%) and fewer Catholics (27% to 35%), although Falkirk and South Lanarkshire are Catholic strongholds. As the percentage for all other denominations is about the national average (26% to 25%) this suggests it is mainly the drift from the Church of Scotland which has caused these areas to be below the churchgoing norm.

The fourth group of six areas (7 Councils) consists of those where church attendance is lowest – the average here is under 8%. Apart from Dumfries and Galloway all these areas are on the eastern side of Scotland. The average percentage of Town churchgoers in these 6 areas is well above the overall average (41% to 32%), although some other parts of Scotland have higher percentages still. Leaving out Aberdeen City, the other 5 areas have only a third of the national average of churchgoers from City Centres, Urban priority Areas, Housing Scheme or Suburban areas (12% to 39%).

Table 3.1: Variations in churchgoing across Scotland

Council(s)	Total attendance, 2002	% of population, 2002	Change 1994-2002 %	Church of Scotland%	Roman Catholic%	All others%
Western Isles[2], Skye & Lochalsh	16,120	39.2	−2	25	13	62
Inverclyde	14,340	17.1	−23	30	54	16
North Lanarkshire	52,360	16.3	−13	27	56	17
Renfrewshire & E. Renfrewshire	40,860	15.6	−19	29	54	17
Glasgow City	82,750	14.2	−19	27	58	15
Shetland Islands	2,890	13.3	−8	33	3	64
East Dunbartonshire	14,260	13.2	−24	43	35	22
Orkney Islands	2,480	12.9	−15	66	6	28
Highland, inc. Argyll & Bute	36,200	12.7	−17	44	22	34
Ayrshire: North, South & East	42,390	11.5	−15	53	25	22
West Dunbartonshire	10,470	11.3	−15	27	55	18
Stirling & Clackmannanshire	14,180	10.6	−17	49	27	24
Moray	9,170	10.5	−18	45	22	33
Perth & Kinross	13,520	10.0	−15	58	17	25
Falkirk	14,100	9.7	−21	35	46	19
Dundee City	14,030	9.7	−21	36	37	27
Aberdeenshire	21,690	9.6	−19	64	13	23
South Lanarkshire	28,870	9.5	−23	37	45	18
City of Edinburgh	40,670	9.0	−19	45	19	36
Scottish Borders	9,730	9.0	−20	63	13	24
Dumfries & Galloway	12,800	8.7	−23	63	14	23
Fife	28,040	8.0	−17	47	23	30
East and Mid Lothian	13,670	8.0	−17	46	30	24
Aberdeen City	16,180	7.7	−16	48	12	40
West Lothian	10,970	6.8	−20	44	35	21
Angus	7,390	6.8	−25	65	12	23
Total All Scotland	570,130	11.2	−18	40	35	25

Figure 3.2: Scottish Councils

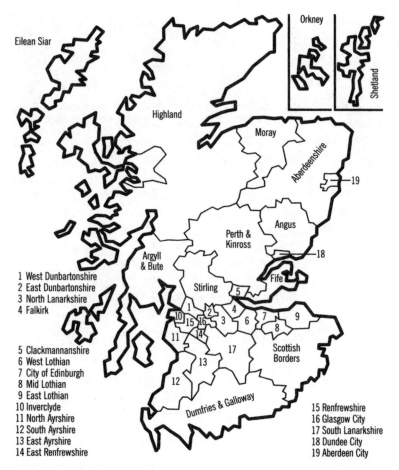

1 West Dunbartonshire
2 East Dunbartonshire
3 North Lanarkshire
4 Falkirk

5 Clackmannanshire
6 West Lothian
7 City of Edinburgh
8 Mid Lothian
9 East Lothian
10 Inverclyde
11 North Ayrshire
12 South Ayrshire
13 East Ayrshire
14 East Renfrewshire

15 Renfrewshire
16 Glasgow City
17 South Lanarkshire
18 Dundee City
19 Aberdeen City

Change in church attendance since 1984

The maps in Figures 3.3, 3.4 and 3.5 show how the percentage of the
population attending church on Sunday has changed between 1984
and 2002. These maps all use the same percentage break points.
Figure 3.2 shows the various Councils by name for ease of reference.

Figure 3.3: Percentage of the population attending church in 1984

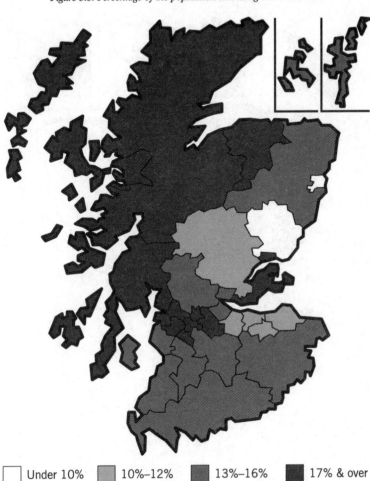

| | Under 10% | | 10%–12% | | 13%–16% | | 17% & over |

While these maps reflect the decreasing percentages coming to church, they also show where the relative strengths of church attendance are located, and how these have remained despite decreasing numbers. The dominance of the Western Isles (Eilean Siar), Skye and Lochalsh remains throughout, essentially because of the Free Church of Scotland.

Figure 3.4: Percentage of the population attending church in 1994

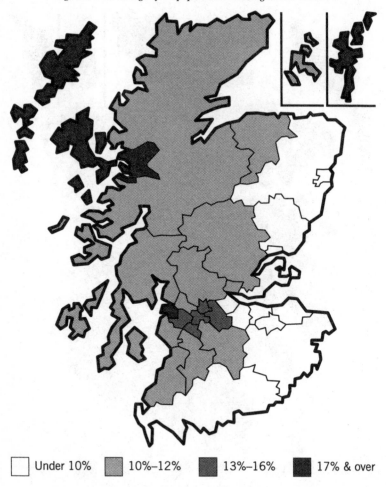

| Under 10% | 10%–12% | 13%–16% | 17% & over |

The recent protests about a Sunday air or boat link between the Western Isles and the mainland reinforce the importance of faith (as expressed in Sunday observance) seen here in these areas.

The importance of Glasgow and much of the old Strathclyde area can also be seen, although the dominance is less. This strength comes from the Roman Catholic Church.

under 10%   10-12.9%   13-16.8%   17% & over

The recent protests about a Sunday air or boat link between the Western Isles and the mainland reinforce the importance of faith (as expressed in Sunday observance) seen here in these areas.

The importance of Glasgow and much of the old Strathclyde area can also be seen, although the dominance is less. This strength comes from the Roman Catholic Church.

ERRATUM

Please substitute this page for page 40.

Figure 3.4: Percentage of the population attending church in 1994

| | Under 10% | | 10%–12% | | 13%–16% | | 17% & over |

The recent protests about a Sunday air or boat link between the Western Isles and the mainland reinforce the importance of faith (as expressed in Sunday observance) seen here in these areas.

The importance of Glasgow and much of the old Strathclyde area can also be seen, although the dominance is less. This strength comes from the Roman Catholic Church.

Figure 3.5: Percentage of the population attending church in 2002

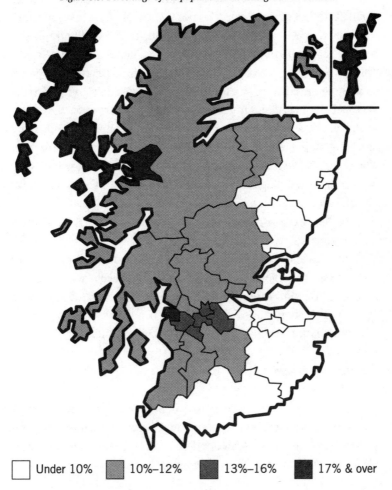

☐ Under 10% ▨ 10%–12% ▨ 13%–16% ■ 17% & over

A North West-South East strength-weakness also clearly emerges, and is especially pronounced in the 2002 map, Figure 3.5. In one of the Focus Groups someone said, "Churches in the west are much more friendly than those in the east", which is an interesting observation commented on further in Chapter 10. This suggests that some churches need to have better welcoming procedures.

There are 13 Councils in the "white" area in Figure 3.5 and 19 Councils in the other areas. The population of these two groups of Councils is almost identical – 2.52 million and 2.54 million respectively. The population density however is quite different. In the "white" area there are 670 people per square kilometre (despite it containing the cities of Aberdeen, Dundee and Edinburgh which are all much higher than this average figure), whereas in the "non-white" area there are 990 people per square kilometre (despite this area containing Argyll & Bute, Highland and the Western Isles which are all much lower). Does the fact that the "non-white" density is half as great again have anything to do with the North West-South East divide?

In the previous Census reports, Angus and Perth & Kinross were combined into Tayside: Other (that is, outside of Dundee). With this area now split into their respective Councils, it can be seen that Angus has the lowest percentage of church attendance in Scotland, a point formerly held by Aberdeen City! This lowest percentage is shared by West Lothian which likewise had only 6.8% of its population attending church on a Sunday in 2002.

Variations by denomination

Detailed maps of the percentage of population in each Council attending church in 1984, 1994 and 2002 by denomination are given in *Religious Trends,* No 4, in Section 2 in full colour. The pertinent elements which emerge from those maps are:

• *Church of Scotland:* Strong in the Western Isles (Eilean Siar), Skye and Lochalsh. Weak in the central belt between Glasgow and Edinburgh, but also in Aberdeen City, Angus and Moray. 1984 to 1994 saw decline everywhere except in the City of Edinburgh and North Lanarkshire. 1994 to 2002 saw declines of 10% or over across all of Scotland.

- *Roman Catholic Church:* Strong in urban areas, especially the former Strathclyde region immediately around Glasgow, and Dundee, but not in Aberdeen City or the City of Edinburgh. Weak also in the Borders and the Tayside area generally. Remains relatively strong in East and West Dunbartonshire, Falkirk, South Lanarkshire and the Western Isles (Eilean Siar), Skye and Lochalsh. Has seen decline of at least 10% in all parts of Scotland in the late 1990s except Perth & Kinross and the Western Isles.

- *Independent Churches:* Strong in the south of Scotland, the former Grampian Region, and the Orkney and Shetland Islands. Remain strong, despite recent decline, in the different Ayrshire and Lanarkshire Councils. Have seen growth in the most recent period especially in Aberdeen City, Perth & Kinross, West Dunbartonshire, West Lothian and the Western Isles (Eilean Siar), Skye and Lochalsh.

- *Smaller denominations:* Particularly strong in Inverclyde, Moray and the Shetland Islands (because of the Methodists). Weak in the south of Scotland, the Orkneys and the Western Isles (Eilean Siar), Skye and Lochalsh. However they grew more than 10% in this latter area between 1994 and 2002, and also in Aberdeenshire, Falkirk, Inverclyde, North Lanarkshire, Renfrewshire & East Renfrewshire and West Dunbartonshire.

- *Baptists:* Particularly strong in the City of Edinburgh (where the 700 attendance at Charlotte Chapel Baptist Church is a major contribution to their strength), and also in Moray, and the Orkney and Shetland Islands. However in the late 1990s they have seen decline in Moray, although continued growth in the Orkney and Shetland Islands. They have grown more than 10% in Perth & Kinross, Stirling & Clackmannanshire, all of Lothian (West, Mid and East) except Edinburgh, Inverclyde and Dumfries & Galloway.

- *Other Presbyterian Churches:* Very strong in the Highlands (with Argyll & Bute) and the Western Islands (Eilean Siar), Skye and Lochalsh. They also have significant strength in Aberdeen City, Dundee City, East and West Dunbartonshire, the Orkney and

Table 3.6: Other geographical comparisons

| | Finance in past year | | | Population per church | | By 2010, our church will have... | | | | |
| | Increased | Remained stable | Decreased | 1984 | 2002 | Grown significantly | Grown a little | Remained stable | Declined | Closed |
Council(s)	%	%	%			%	%	%	%	%
Western Isles[2], Skye & Lochalsh	68	21	11	270	290	24	54	11	11	0
Inverclyde	71	19	10	1,800	1,420	43	24	14	19	0
North Lanarkshire	62	27	11	1,580	1,520	19	37	18	24	2
Renfrewshire & E. Renfrewshire	65	29	6	2,100	1,720	21	37	18	22	2
Glasgow City	59	26	15	1,670	1,460	21	34	19	24	2
Shetland Islands	49	49	2	380	340	16	33	23	28	0
East Dunbartonshire	74	17	9	2,020	1,890	28	43	24	5	0
Orkney Islands	29	62	9	420	440	4	17	35	44	0
Highland, inc. Argyll & Bute	58	34	8	530	550	14	41	24	18	3
Ayrshire: North, South & East	67	23	10	1,410	1,330	16	37	20	25	2
West Dunbartonshire	61	21	18	1,640	1,500	8	42	27	23	0
Stirling & Clackmannanshire	70	27	3	1,200	1,150	16	46	25	11	2
Moray	79	15	6	750	900	16	51	24	9	0
Perth & Kinross	59	37	4	960	920	18	35	33	12	2
Falkirk	67	33	0	1,760	1,570	22	37	23	13	5
Dundee City	57	32	11	1,480	1,460	27	39	16	16	2
Aberdeenshire	63	30	7	970	1,160	19	40	26	12	3
South Lanarkshire	67	29	4	2,120	1,860	11	44	23	21	1
City of Edinburgh	63	30	7	1,900	1,870	20	36	23	20	1
Scottish Borders	63	32	5	680	720	25	34	26	11	4
Dumfries & Galloway	52	40	8	830	860	10	31	24	26	9
Fife	64	26	10	1,400	1,360	22	41	13	22	2
East and Mid Lothian	71	22	7	1,430	1,430	34	38	14	14	0
Aberdeen City	55	34	11	1,870	1,770	26	34	19	21	0
West Lothian	73	17	10	1,930	1,890	21	45	10	21	3
Angus	56	37	7	1,140	1,080	7	43	25	25	0
Total All Scotland	62	30	8	1,240	1,220	20	37	22	19	2

Table 3.7: Other geographical variations by church attendance

	Finance in past year			Population per church		By 2010, our church will have...				
	Increased	Remained stable	Decreased	1984	2002	Grown significantly	Grown a little	Remained stable	Declined	Closed
Council(s)	%	%	%			%	%	%	%	%
Attendance well above normal	62	26	12	1,630	1,430	22	36	18	22	2
Attendance above normal	63	27	10	1,170	1,110	16	39	23	20	2
Attendance below normal	65	30	5	1,500	1,460	18	40	24	16	2
Attendance well below normal	62	29	9	1,450	1,420	22	38	17	21	2
Total All Scotland	62	30	8	1,240	1,220	20	37	22	19	2

Shetland Islands, Perth & Kinross and Stirling and Clackmannanshire. Have seen decline in recent years in Fife, the Grampian area and much of the central urban belt.

- *Episcopal Churches:* Strong in the City of Edinburgh and the Highlands where they have held their position, and the Scottish Borders. Between 1994 and 2002 they grew more than 10% in West Dunbartonshire, but have seen decline especially in the east and south of Scotland, and also the Western Isles, Skye & Lochalsh.

Other geographical variations

Table 3.6 gives other data by Council or area[3], using the same order as in Table 3.1 for ease of comparison.

How do the figures in Table 3.6 vary according to the percentage who attend church? If the average figures are worked out for each group, then the numbers illustrated in Figure 3.7 emerge.

Interestingly, there is no relationship between financial change and church attendance. About three-fifths, 62%, of churches said their financial giving had increased in the past year, but this did not vary by whether their attendance had increased or decreased. This perhaps implies that in declining churches the amount given per person might have increased. Presumably expenses stay roughly the same so they have to give more to keep going. That they do so is a sign of their commitment.

The churches whose attendance had increased most had the largest catchment per church, that is, they are largely located in urban areas. The decrease between 1984 and 2002 is because Glasgow City is in the top group, and its population has changed with the boundary changes.

Churches which are in areas where attendance has grown are positive about the future – 58% said their churches could be expected to grow either a little or significantly by 2010. Churches in areas where attendance was just above normal were marginally less optimistic, 55%. However, 58% of churches in areas where it was just below normal felt they would grow, and 60% of churches in areas where attendance was below normal. This suggests that the worse the actual attendance change (outside best performing areas) the greater the optimism for growth. Does this reflect being out of touch with reality or a commitment to turn things round?

So what does all this say?

This chapter has shown:

- Five areas are seeing church attendance at much higher levels than across Scotland generally. These are where the Roman Catholic Church is especially strong and also the Western Isles (Eilean Siar), Skye and Lochalsh where the Free Church of Scotland is strong. Two out of five in the population, 39%, in the Western Isles, Skye and Lochalsh attend church on Sunday.
- There are six areas where attendance is well below the norm. These are on the eastern side of Scotland and Dumfries and Galloway. Angus and West Lothian have the lowest church attendance in Scotland at 6.8%, which is only three-fifths of the normal of 11.2%.

- The western and north western parts of Scotland have maintained a higher churchgoing rate than the eastern and southern parts over the years 1984 to 2002.
- Financial change is not associated with church attendance change.
- It is possible that optimism for growth is inversely related to actual church attendance, outside the areas of highest attendance.

NOTES

[1] In most of the combined areas, the number of churchgoers is too few to justify reasonably accurate analysis when broken down by these four control variables.

[2] Eilean Siar in Gaelic.

[3] This data is not repeated in *Religious Trends*.

4) Churchgoing by age and gender

One generation from extinction! In one sense, such a phrase is always true of the church. If we fail to pass on our message to the next generation, the church will die. But in the postmodern world we are increasingly seeing not only the children of non-churchgoing families failing to attend church, but sometimes even the children of churchgoing parents. John Wesley said, "If religion is not extended to the children, what will be the outcome?" What, indeed?

Attendance by age-group over time, 1984 to 2002

Table 4.1 gives the basic numbers by age-group emerging from the various Scottish Church Censuses, which are illustrated in Figure 4.2:

Table 4.1: Numbers attending church by age-group, 1984–2002

Year	Under 15	15–19	20–29	30–44	45–64	65 and over	Total
1984	213,430	42,680	76,830	128,060	204,890	187,810	**853,700**
% change	*–42*	*–19*	*–28*	*–8*	*–9*	*–8*	*–19*
1994	124,400	34,560	55,290	117,490	186,600	172,780	**691,120**
% change	*–21*	*–31*	*–34*	*–31*	*–16*	*+1*	*–18*
2002	98,420	23,800	36,710	80,820	156,640	173,740	**570,130**

It may be seen from both the Table and the diagram that the age-groups with the largest percentages leaving between 1994 and 2002 were for those aged between 15 and 44. The groups where the largest numbers left were for those in their 20s (nearly 20,000), those

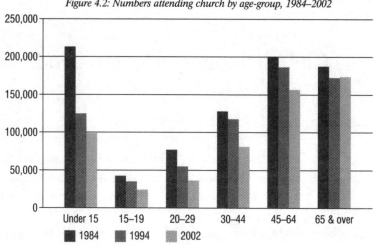

Figure 4.2: Numbers attending church by age-group, 1984–2002

aged 30 to 44 (nearly 40,000) and for those 45 to 64 (about 30,000). While each of these is important, the latter two groups are especially crucial since many of these people will have children, and if the parents leave, their children are likely to follow if not today then tomorrow when they are older (as other research has shown[1]).

It may also be seen that the number of churchgoers aged 65 or over has slightly increased when all other age-groups have decreased. The same trend was seen amongst English churchgoers 1989 to 1998.

Comparison with the population

The figures in Table 4.1 are expressed as percentages for each age-group in Table 4.3, and the population figures are given for comparison.

The increasing percentage of Scottish churchgoers who are 65 and over should be noted since this age-group is not increasing in anything like the same proportions in the population as a whole. In 2002, almost a third, 31%, of churchgoers were 65 or over, which is

Table 4.3: Percentages in church and population, by age-group, 1984–2002

Age-group	Churchgoers			Population		
	1984 %	1994 %	2002 %	1984 %	1994 %	2002 %
Under 15	25	18	17	21	19	18
15–19	5	5	4	9	6	4
20–29	9	8	6	15	16	13
30–44	15	17	14	19	21	24
45–64	24	27	28	22	23	24
65 & over	22	25	31	14	15	15
Base	853,700	691,120	570,130	5.1m	5.1m	5.1m

twice the proportion of elderly in the total population. This means that 23% of people 65 and over go to church in Scotland (a percentage much higher than any other age-group[2]) but it has obvious concerns for the future.

The declining proportions of churchgoers are among those under 45. The percentage has dropped one point for those under 20, and two points for those in their 20s (quite a large proportion), in both of which the proportions in the population have also lessened (especially of those in their 20s).

However while the percentage of churchgoers aged 30 to 44 has decreased especially since 1994, in the population as a whole this age-group has increased, the only age-group where population and church attendance move in opposite directions. Losses here are therefore especially important, as they are contrary to what might have been expected. This issue was explored in the Focus Groups, which are reported in Chapter 10.

Those under 15

The Scottish Church Census took place after the results of the 1998 English Church Census were known. One of the key findings of the English study was a drastic drop in the number of children attending church. It was therefore natural to ask if this was also true in

Scotland. Accordingly the number of children attending was broken down for the first time into those under 12 and those aged 12 to 14:
• 13% of churchgoers were under 12 (6% male, 7% female), and
• 4% were aged 12 to 14 (2% male, 2% female).

The respective percentages in the population as a whole are 14% (7% male, 7% female) and 4% (2% male, 2% female). Thus those aged 12 to 14 are as proportionate in the church as they are in the population (and in both genders), something which is not true in England. This indicates that while the numbers of children in church have declined, those aged 12 to 14 have not dropped out more than those younger.

The Scottish churches are therefore at this time relatively successful in retaining their children, even though overall numbers are decreasing. Perhaps this is partly the Scottish tradition of churchgoing, the family togetherness, and the enjoyment of Sunday activities (often in a Bible Class, Sunday School or perhaps Youth service).

However, as already mentioned, the decreasing numbers of parents is bound to impact child and teenage church attendance in the future, and finding ways of addressing this concern would seem to be an urgent strategic consideration.

Churchgoers by age and gender

The figures in Table 4.1 may be broken down by gender; these are given in Table 4.4, in which the total of "Male" and "Female" adds to the appropriate total.

There are a number of areas where the figures in Table 4.4 reveal fresh factors not shown by the combined figures given in Table 4.1. Some of these are as follows:
• Between 1984 and 1994 girls under 15 left the church faster than boys, but between 1994 and 2002 boys left faster than girls.
• In both decades women between 15 and 40 have left the church in much greater proportions than men.

- Women aged 45 to 64 have also left the church in much greater numbers between 1994 and 2002, but did not between 1984 and 1994.
- The experience of the older churchgoers, 65 and over, is quite different! More men came to church in the 1984 to 1994 period. The numbers between 1994 and 2002 have hardly changed; normal mortality will be an important factor here and could well account for the decrease. These are net figures, not gross, and are the difference between gains and losses. Were the male gains to be considered apart from deaths they might well have been positive between 1994 and 2002. Older women on the other hand decreased between 1984 and 1994 but have increased slightly between 1994 and 2002. Were there a particularly large number of older women who died in the earlier period?

Table 4.4: Numbers attending church by age-group and gender, 1984–2002

Male	Under 15	15–19	20–29	30–44	45–64	65/65+	Total
1984	93,910	17,070	25,610	42,690	76,830	59,760	**315,870**
% change	−36	−7	−19	−3	−10	+4	−15
1994	60,200	15,820	20,740	41,470	69,110	62,200	**269,540**
% change	−28	−28	−18	−26	−9	−2	−16
2002	43,610	11,400	17,100	30,510	62,710	60,720	**226,050**
Female	Under 15	15–19	20–29	30–44	45–64	65/65+	Total
1984	119,520	25,610	51,220	85,370	128,060	128,050	**537,830**
% change	−46	−27	−33	−11	−8	−14	−22
1994	64,200	18,740	34,550	76,020	117,490	110,580	**421,580**
% change	−15	−34	−43	−34	−20	+2	−18
2002	54,810	12,400	19,610	50,310	93,930	113,020	**344,080**

The balance of the genders varies also, as shown in Table 4.5, where the male percentage in a given age-group is given. The female percentage is simply obtained by subtracting each from 100%.

Apart from the youngest and oldest age-groups, the proportion of men in Scottish churches has increased across all age-groups from

Table 4.5: Gender balance by age-group, male percentage, 1984–2002

Male %	Under 15	15–19	20–29	30–44	45–64	65/65+	Total
1984	44	40	33	33	37	32	37
1994	48	46	38	35	37	36	39
2002	44	48	47	38	40	35	40

15 to 64 between 1984 and 2002. This is not because more men have joined the church but because more women have left.

The figures show a serious trend because it is often women in these middle age-groups who help to run the many church activities, supporting church life and outreach into the local communities.

Numbers leaving church

Using the figures in Table 4.4 it is very easy to construct the number by which churchgoers have dropped by age and gender in the two periods 1984–1994 and 1994–2002. These are shown in Figure 4.6.

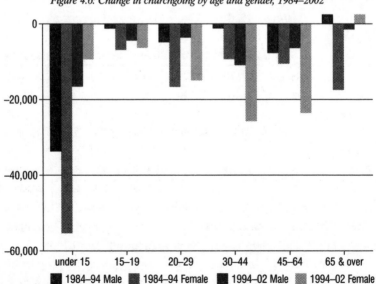

Figure 4.6: Change in churchgoing by age and gender, 1984–2002

The left hand pair of columns for each age-group in Figure 4.6 relate to the earlier period 1984 to 1994, and the right hand pair the later period 1994 to 2002. Many children left in the earlier period, but in the later period the large numbers of women leaving, many more than men, are readily seen.

More women than men also left aged 15 to 44 in the earlier period, 1984 to 1994. The new feature in this latest study is women 45 and over who are leaving much more than men, and the much larger number of women aged 30 to 44 who have left in these eight years than in the previous decade.

Churchgoing by age-group and denomination

How do the figures vary by denomination? Table 4.7 gives the basic numbers for 2002 by denomination, and Figure 4.8 shows the proportion in each age-group. Those wanting similar information for earlier years, and also broken down by gender, will find the relevant percentages in *Religious Trends*.[3]

Table 4.7: Sunday church attendance by age-group and denomination, 2002

Denomination	Under 15	15–19	20–29	30–44	45–64	65/65+	Total	Avge Age
Church of Scotland	35,450	6,140	10,280	24,660	64,780	87,190	**228,500**	51
Roman Catholic	37,400	11,120	14,170	34,390	56,570	48,460	**202,110**	44
Independent	8,500	2,700	4,050	6,710	11,250	11,800	**45,010**	44
Smaller denominations	4,580	1,140	2,580	4,580	7,450	8,310	**28,640**	46
Baptist	4,970	1,240	2,980	4,960	6,210	4,470	**24,830**	40
Other Presbyterian	4,880	890	1,330	2,880	5,100	7,090	**22,170**	45
Episcopal	2,640	570	1,320	2,640	5,280	6,420	**18,870**	50
Total All Scotland	**98,420**	**23,800**	**36,710**	**80,820**	**156,640**	**173,740**	**570,130**	**47**

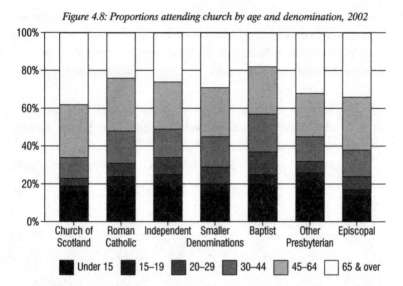

Figure 4.8: Proportions attending church by age and denomination, 2002

The Table and diagram show the relatively small proportion of children who are in the Episcopal Church (14% against 17% overall). Likewise the small proportion of those in their 20s in the Church of Scotland (4% to 6% overall), but much larger proportions in the Baptist (12%) and the Independent and Smaller Denominations (9% each). The Baptists have a higher percentage of those aged 30 to 44 (20%) than other denominations; the average is 14%, but the Church of Scotland only has 11%.

Other Presbyterians have the smallest percentage of those aged 45 to 64 (23% to 28% overall). The largest variations, however, occur amongst the oldest, 65 and over. The overall average is 31%, but the Church of Scotland has 38%, the Baptists only 18%, with the Roman Catholics (24%) and the Independents (26%) in between.

The Church of Scotland attenders have the highest average age, 51, against the overall average of 47. The Episcopal Church has the next highest average, 50, and these are the only two groups above the average. Baptists have the lowest average age at 40, which probably helps explain why they are growing – they have more younger people, and presumably therefore more energy, and in particular more people at the critical middle age-groups who are able to help with the running of church activities.

Who are these different age-groups?

The people of varying ages who go to church in Scotland represent different generations, which have been identified by various names. As it may be helpful to give these, they are listed in Table 4.9:

Table 4.9 Six generations of Scottish people

Generation	Other names	Years of birth	Age range in 2003	Scottish population in 2001[4]	
Seniors		1926 and earlier	77+	287,031	(6%)
Builders	Boosters, Maturity	1927–45	58–76	891,029	(18%)
Boomers	Baby Boomers	1946–64	39–57	1,322,477	(26%)
Busters	Generation X	1965–83	20–38	1,337,319	(26%)
Mosaics	Generation Y	1984–02	1–19	1,172,053	(23%)
Kaleidoscopes	Generation Z	2003–21	Under 1	52,102	(1%)

In 2001, exactly half the Scottish population were 39 or over and half 38 or under. The topology given above originally came from the United States and centred around their "Baby Boom" people, a well-above-average number who were born in the late 1940s. Britain experienced a similar "boom" in births in the late 1950s and early 1960s, and thus conveniently have a group born in the same period as America. These "boomers" as they were called ("baby" being dropped fairly quickly) were then seen as a generation, and their children (who broke, or bust, the boom) were called "Busters", while their parents were called different names of which perhaps "Builders" is the most acceptable.

The "Busters" were also called the Millennium Generation, as the generation which would reach adulthood at the start of the new millennium, or "Beepers" as they grew up with the new technology.

A much more contemporary term quickly caught on in the early 1990s from a book by Douglas Coupland[5] – the X Generation or Generation X. Many other books and articles[6] have followed about this generation.

Their children somewhat naturally are called Generation Y, but they have also been called other names, of which "Mosaics" is the most common, since their world view is made up of scattered pieces each with part of the total picture, like a Roman mosaic. *Their* children, Generation Z, may also be called "Kaleidoscopes", since they are likely to make more than one picture (or world view) with the pieces they put together.

The value of this kind of topology is that it can conveniently be used to describe some of the different characteristics for each generation. This has been undertaken in detail, from several sources, in the book *Reaching and Keeping Tweenagers*[7], but one Table summarising some of the key characteristics may be of value to church leaders thinking through how different generations may be encouraged to come to church.

Table 4.10: Generational characteristics

Characteristic	Builders (58–76)	Boomers (39–57)	Gen X (20–38)	Mosaics (1–19)
Respect...	Status	Competence	Openness	Involvement
Support	Can manage without it	Like it	Need it	Constant mobile use
Work	Happy to do any job	More specialist	Look at team first	Own own business
Church	Attend out of habit	Like to use their gifts	Attend when I feel like it	What's Christianity?
Think...	Linearly and logically		Creatively	Fragmentally

Thus, for example, while Builders, many of whom are now retired, were happy to do any job (they needed the money!), Boomers preferred jobs which fitted their gifting or speciality (they could usually do a good job therefore). Gen Xers, on the other hand, want to know with whom they will be working first, rather than details about the job itself – company counts! Mosaics don't mind working in teams, but prefer independence, or at least the ability to do things the way they want, and running their own organisation fits this very neatly.

This chapter has shown that the Scottish church has seen large numbers of the Boomers and Gen X age-groups leave the church. What would Gen Xers appreciate about a church? Not being expected to come every week(!), leaders admitting when they have made mistakes, being involved with others and doing things together as a team, being allowed to make creative suggestions, and encouraged to keep on keeping on. Boomers on the other hand would like to be asked to do something which matched their particular gifts, would respect those who were doing things professionally and would expect to work to similar standards.

What of the future?

In 1980, 17.1% of Scotland's population attended church on a Sunday. By 2002, just over 20 years later, this had dropped to 11.2%, two-thirds of what it had been. If present trends continue, especially the loss of women, then in almost 20 years time, in 2020, the percentage could be down 6.8%, only three-fifths of what it was in 2002. As already noted, the rate of decline is increasing. This 6.8% is still higher than the anticipated English percentage of 4% by then.

How far is this drop just because of normal mortality, especially as many churchgoers are elderly? It is really only among those 65 and over that the number of deaths becomes important. The numbers leaving in younger age-groups naturally include some who die but so many are leaving for other reasons that the death rates, estimated from Life Tables and included within the percentages in the previous paragraph, have little impact outside those aged 65 and over. They impact here because so many churchgoers are elderly.

Table 4.11 breaks down this forecast in more detail.

Table 4.11: Estimated proportions attending church in Scotland, 2005–2020

Year	Under 15	15–19	20–29	30–44	45–64	65/65+	Base	Avge Age	% of pop
2002	17	4	6	14	28	31	**570,130**	47	11.2
2005	14	4	6	15	29	32	**510,900**	49	10.3
2010	9	4	4	15	32	36	**432,200**	53	8.7
2020	5	3	3	14	35	40	**331,200**	56	6.8

If present trends continue the number of children attending church will continue to drop, and the proportion of those 45 or over in the church steadily increase. If the figures in Table 4.11 come to reality, then by 2020 three-quarters, 75%, of churchgoers will be 45 or over, naturally increasing the average age. The proportion of men in the church steadily increases from the 40% in 2002 to 43% by 2020 – if women continue to leave the church more than men.

Table 4.11 does not present a happy picture, and calls for urgent and strategic action by church leaders of all denominations now in order that the forecasts it contains will NOT come true.

So what does all this say?

This chapter has looked at the age and gender of churchgoers. It has shown:

- The number of children under 15 attending church fell rapidly between 1984 and 1994 but has continued to decline at 2.9% per annum.
- However the proportions of those leaving between 15 and 64 from 1994 to 2002 have all accelerated against the decreases seen between 1984 and 1994.
- The key reason for this has been the extra numbers of women leaving the church.

- The number of people attending church aged 65 or over has marginally increased between 1994 and 2002 (as it did in England). There were slightly more men of this age in church in 1994 than 1984, and slightly more women in church in 2002 than in 1994.
- Compared with the population the church has twice as many people 65 and over, and only half the percentage of those in their 20s.
- Because women are leaving the church at a faster rate than men, the proportion of men in the church has increased from 37% in 1984 to 40% in 2002. This increase is seen across all age groups between 15 and 64.
- The Church of Scotland (51) and the Episcopal Church (50) have the highest percentage of those 65 and over, and consequently the highest average age (shown in brackets). The Baptists on the other hand have the highest percentage of all denominations of people aged 30 to 44, and the lowest average age (40).
- The different generations need to be reached in different ways, each relevant to the culture of that age-group.
- If the present trends continue, future Scottish church life becomes more difficult, as the church has growing numbers of elderly attenders (the average age goes up to 56 by 2020), and sees an increasing smaller percentage of the population involved (under 7% by 2020).

This is a bleak picture, and will not make pleasant reading for the many ministers and lay people doing their best to keep things going in their churches. It would be wrong, however, not look at the trends implicit in the data. Urgent, strategic action is needed in churches of all denominations if these forecasts are not to become reality.

NOTES

[1] See, for example, the results of the analysis of religious groups in Switzerland given in Werner Haug's article in *The demographic characteristics of national minorities in certain European states,* edited Werner Haug et al, Population Studies No 31, Volume 2, Council of Europe Directorate General III, Social Cohesion, Strasbourg, January 2000, and quoted in Table 1.6.3 of *Religious Trends,* No 3, 2002/2003, Christian Research, London, 2001.

[2] The percentages for the other age-groups are: 10% Under 12, 11% 12 to 14, 11% 15 to 19, 5% 20 to 29, 7% 30 to 44 and 13% 45 to 64.

[3] *Religious Trends,* No 4, 2003/2004, Christian Research, London, Pages 12.30 to 12.36.

[4] *2001 Population Report Scotland,* Registrar General for Scotland, Edinburgh, 2002, Table 1.

[5] *Generation X, Tales from an accelerated culture,* D Coupland, St Martin's Press, USA, 1991.

[6] For example, *From Separation to Synergy, receiving the richness of Generation X,* Kath Donovan, Zadok Paper S106, Zadok Institute, Winter 2000; *Generation NeXt,* George Barna, Regal Books, Ventura, California, USA, 1995; *Generation X, Attitudes and Lifestyles,* Survey Report, Peter Brierley, Christian Research, March 2001; *Why do they do that – Understanding Teenagers,* Nick Pollard, Lion, 1998; *Boomers, Xers, and Other Strangers,* Dr Rick & Kathy Hicks, Tyndale, 1999; *Generation Y, young, gifted and self-centred,* article by Mark Henderson in *The Times,* 14/11/98.

[7] *Reaching and Keeping Tweenagers,* Peter Brierley, Christian Research, London, 2003, Chapter 1.

5) Churchgoing by churchmanship and environment

What people believe is important! "Churchmanship" is a rather quaint term which is often of great significance to clergy, but less well understood by lay people. Studies of whole congregations usually show a range of churchmanships among the attenders, even if the majority align themselves with the description suggested by their minister. Given a choice, Protestants tend to go to a church which appeals to them, or has something specific they are looking for, such as good provision for their children, or within walking distance for an elderly person. An identical question on churchmanship was used in both the 1994 and 2002 Censuses.

Where people live is also important, and may affect their choice of, and attitudes towards, church. Churchgoing in a rural environment may be quite different from that in an inner city. A church's environment was requested in 1994 against one of eight categories, and has been used again in the 2002 analysis since for the very large majority it will not have changed.

Ministers were invited to indicate the churchmanship of their congregation by ticking up to three boxes (out of nine). From the grouping of their responses they were allocated into one of six categories[1]: Broad, Catholic, Evangelical, Liberal, Low Church and Reformed. The Evangelical group was further sub-divided into Reformed, Mainstream and Charismatic Evangelical.

Growth

Growth was only seen in three groups when 1994 attendance was

compared with 2002:
- By denominational group, Baptists grew 1%
- By age/gender, those aged 65 and over grew 1%
- By churchmanship, Mainstream Evangelicals grew 19%.

This last is so much greater than the first two that it cannot help but be noticed. It is shown in Figure 5.1. The same finding was however also true of the English survey of 1998.

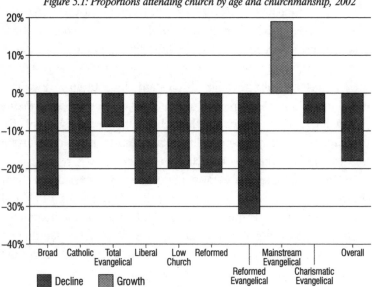

Figure 5.1: Proportions attending church by age and churchmanship, 2002

Churchmanship by denomination

Churchmanship varied by denomination, as would be expected. The basic numbers and how they changed are given in Table 5.2, but it can be misleading – for example it looks like a massive decline of Liberal Baptists but these numbers only relate to a few churches, and likewise for Broad Independents.

Table 5.2: Churchmanship by denomination, 1994 and 2002

Denomination		Broad	Catholic	Evangelical	Liberal	Low Church	Reformed	Total
Church of	*1994*	69,520	1,690	67,180	32,610	23,270	98,900	**293,170**
Scotland	*+/– (%)*	*–27*	*–35*	*–18*	*–20*	*–22*	*–22*	*–22*
	2002	51,090	1,100	55,100	26,030	18,040	77,140	**228,500**
Roman	*1994*	5,700	214,940	2,790	24,180	2,110	0	**249,720**
Catholic	*+/– (%)*	*–30*	*–17*	*+11*	*–41*	*–5*	–	*–19*
	2002	3,980	178,870	3,100	14,160	2,000	0	**202,110**
Independent	*1994*	580	0	42,170	2,840	630	1,800	**48,020**
	+/– (%)	*+17*	–	*–5*	*–23*	*–5*	*–19*	*–6*
	1994	680	0	40,070	2,200	600	1,460	**45,010**
Smaller	*1994*	3,830	660	19,970	4,900	1,850	810	**32,020**
denomin-	*+/– (%)*	*–30*	*–62*	*–5*	*–16*	*+1*	*+5*	*–11*
ations	*2002*	2,670	250	18,880	4,130	1,860	850	**28,640**
Baptist	*1994*	0	0	24,150	380	0	0	**24,530**
	+/– (%)	–	–	*+2*	*–18*	–	–	*+1*
	2002	0	0	24,520	310	0	0	**24,830**
Other	*1994*	130	0	18,740	80	170	4,190	**23,310**
Presbyterian	*+/– (%)*	*+31*	–	*–8*	*–12*	*–24*	*+7*	*–5*
	2002	170	0	17,300	70	130	4,500	**22,170**
Episcopal	*1994*	4,340	4,200	3,960	4,310	1,670	1,870	**20,350**
	+/– (%)	*–37*	*–12*	*+7*	*+36*	*–25*	*–41*	*–7*
	2002	2,750	3,680	4,230	5,860	1,250	1,100	**18,870**
Total	*1994*	**84,100**	**221,490**	**178,960**	**69,300**	**29,700**	**107,570**	**691,120**
All	*+/– (%)*	*–27*	*–17*	*–9*	*–24*	*–20*	*–21*	*–18*
Scotland	*2002*	**61,340**	**183,900**	**163,200**	**52,760**	**23,880**	**85,050**	**570,130**

Table 5.2 shows the various trends in churchmanship across the different denominations, the most surprising of which are perhaps the growth of Evangelicals in a very small number of Roman Catholic churches, and the growth of Liberals in the Scottish Episcopal Church given their decline everywhere else. The Table can

Table 5.3: Evangelicals by denomination, 1994 and 2002

Denomination		Charismatic Evangelical	Mainstream Evangelical	Reformed Evangelical	Total Evangelical
Church of	*1994*	5,070	11,320	50,790	**67,180**
Scotland	*+/– (%)*	*–16*	*+86*	*–41*	*–18*
	2002	4,240	21,030	29,830	**55,100**
Roman	*1994*	0	2,790	0	**2,790**
Catholic	*+/– (%)*	–	*+11*	–	*+11*
	2002	0	3,100	0	**3,100**
Independent	*1994*	13,360	22,920	5,890	**42,170**
	+/– (%)	*–19*	*+8*	*–24*	*–5*
	1994	10,840	24,770	4,460	**40,070**
Smaller	*1994*	7,360	9,930	2,680	**19,970**
denomin-	*+/– (%)*	*–2*	*–1*	*–32*	*–5*
ations	*2002*	7,240	9,810	1,830	**18,880**
Baptist	*1994*	3,350	16,300	4,500	**24,150**
	+/– (%)	*+20*	*+1*	*–11*	*+2*
	2002	4,010	16,490	4,020	**24,830**
Other	*1994*	0	2,810	15,930	**23,310**
Presbyterian	*+/– (%)*	–	*+32*	*–15*	*–5*
	2002	0	3,700	13,600	**22,170**
Episcopal	*1994*	2,050	1,770	140	**20,350**
	+/– (%)	*+9*	*–5*	*+129*	*–7*
	2002	2,230	1,680	320	**18,870**
Total	*1994*	**31,190**	**67,840**	**79,930**	**178,960**
All	*+/– (%)*	*–8*	*+19*	*–32*	*–9*
Scotland	*2002*	**28,560**	**80,580**	**54,060**	**163,200**

be read across the rows to give the proportions of each churchmanship within each denomination and how they changed between 1994
and 2002. The proportions within each denomination of each
churchmanship can be seen down the columns. The first of these
analyses is given in *Religious Trends* No 4[2], and is not repeated here.
As the main movement in churchmanship has been in one branch of

Evangelicalism, Table 5.3 breaks down the total Evangelicals given in Table 5.2 into its three components, and Table 5.4 the proportions of each churchmanship (using the three strands of Evangelicals) within each denomination. In Table 5.4 "n/a" means there are no churchgoers in that churchmanship/denomination category and "*" means that the percentage is under 0.5%.

Table 5.4: Churchmanship proportions by denomination, 1994 and 2002

Denomination	Broad %	Catholic %	Evangelical: Charismatic %	Evangelical: Mainstream %	Evangelical: Reformed %	Liberal %	Low Church %	Reformed %
1994								
Church of Scot.	83	1	16	17	64	47	78	92
Roman Catholic	7	97	n/a	4	n/a	35	7	n/a
Independent	1	n/a	43	34	7	4	2	1
Smaller denoms.	4	*	24	15	3	7	6	1
Baptist	n/a	n/a	11	24	6	1	n/a	n/a
Other Presbytrn	*	n/a	n/a	4	20	*	1	4
Episcopal	5	2	6	2	*	6	6	2
Base	84,100	221,490	31,190	67,840	79,930	69,300	29,700	107,570
2002								
Church of Scot.	83	1	15	26	55	49	76	91
Roman Catholic	7	97	n/a	4	n/a	27	8	n/a
Independent	1	n/a	38	31	8	4	2	2
Smaller denoms.	4	*	25	12	3	8	8	1
Baptist	n/a	n/a	14	20	8	1	n/a	n/a
Other Presbytrn	*	n/a	n/a	5	25	*	1	5
Episcopal	5	2	8	2	1	11	5	1
Base	61,340	183,900	28,560	80,580	54,060	52,760	23,880	85,050

* = Under 0.5%

Certain churchmanships are closely associated with particular denominations. Those of Broad, Low Church or Reformed theology are especially likely to be found in Church of Scotland congregations, the Catholic persuasion in the Roman Catholic Churches, while Liberals are shared between the Church of Scotland and Roman Catholic. Evangelical Reformed are seen in the Church of Scotland and Other Presbyterian Churches. Charismatic and Mainstream Evangelicals tend to be mostly in the Independent congregations, followed by the Church of Scotland, Smaller Denominations and the Baptists.

Proportions have not changed greatly between 1994 and 2002. The main change has been the increasing number of mainstream Evangelicals within the Church of Scotland.

Churchmanship by age-group

How does churchmanship vary with age? Table 5.5 gives the basic numbers for 2002 by churchmanship, and Figure 5.6 shows the proportion in each age-group. Similar information for 1994, also broken down by gender, is available[3].

Table 5.5: Sunday church attendance by age-group and churchmanship, 2002

Churchmanship	Under 15	15–19	20–29	30–44	45–64	65/65+	Total	Avge Age
Broad	8,850	1,110	1,810	6,670	18,320	24,580	**61,340**	53
Catholic	37,230	11,760	17,400	32,230	47,220	38,060	**183,900**	41
Evan: Charismatic	6,570	2,140	3,780	6,020	6,830	3,220	**28,560**	36
Evan: Mainstream	13,950	3,650	6,200	11,550	21,710	23,520	**80,580**	46
Evan: Reformed	8,200	1,540	1,610	6,640	15,110	20,960	**54,060**	51
Liberal	7,960	950	2,080	5,860	15,490	20,420	**52,760**	52
Low Church	3,300	670	800	2,900	6,850	9,360	**23,880**	52
Reformed	12,360	1,980	3,030	8,950	25,110	33,620	**85,050**	52
Total All Scotland	**98,420**	**23,800**	**36,710**	**80,820**	**156,640**	**173,740**	**570,130**	**47**

Figure 5.6 shows the relatively small proportion of children who are in the Broad, Liberal, Low Church and Reformed groups (respectively 14%, 15%, 14% and 15% against 17% overall). Conversely it also shows the high percentage of people 65 and over

(respectively 40%, 39%, 39% and 40% against 31% overall), seen as well in the high average ages in Table 5.5.

They also show that the "Evangelical" group is split into 3 very different communities. The Reformed Evangelical are very similar to the "Reformed" group, with a low percentage of children and high percentage of older people (15% and 39% respectively) and high average age. The Charismatic Evangelical are the opposite with a high percentage of children and low percentage of older people (23% and 11% respectively), with a very low average age. These two groups are at the opposite ends of a spectrum, with the Mainstream Evangelicals in between. With 17% who are children and 29% 65 and over, they are almost exactly half-way, marginally leaning towards the Charismatics.

The Catholic group, not to be confused with the Roman Catholic Church, are much closer to the younger Charismatics than the older groups, with 20% who are children and 21% who are 65 and over. This can also be seen in their average age, much younger than most of the others.

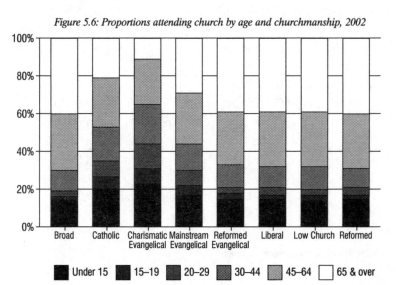

Figure 5.6: Proportions attending church by age and churchmanship, 2002

Church attendance and the environment

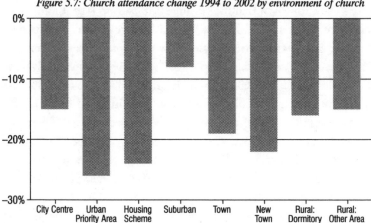

Figure 5.7: Church attendance change 1994 to 2002 by environment of church

As Figure 5.7 indicates, church attendance declined in all environments, dropping least in suburbia and most in Urban Priority Areas (UPAs).

Churchgoing in Scotland was spread across these various environments in 2002 as follows, with 1994 proportions in brackets, which show that the percentages have not changed greatly in the eight years:

- 32% in Towns   (33%)
- 16% in Suburban locations   (14%)
- 15% in Other Rural Areas   (14%)
- 11% on Housing Schemes   (12%)
- 10% in Rural Dormitory Areas   (10%)
- 7% in City Centres   (7%)
- 5% in Urban Priority Areas, and (6%)
- 4% in New Towns.   (4%)

Environment by denomination

Just as certain denominations are stronger in some churchmanships than others, so are some stronger in certain environments. Table 5.8 gives the basic figures on how Sunday church attendance has varied by these two factors between 1994 and 2002.

Table 5.8: Churchmanship by environment and denomination, 1994 and 2002

		City Centre	UPA	Housing Scheme	Suburban	Town	New Town	Rural: Dormitory	Rural: Other	Total
Church of Scotland	94	11,060	14,440	21,700	52,480	93,180	6,860	42,380	51,070	**293,170**
	+/–	–26	–39	–37	–13	–24	–30	–20	–17	**–22**
	02	8,230	8,840	13,740	45,640	71,140	4,790	33,760	42,360	**228,500**
Roman Catholic	94	21,810	18,530	50,970	25,220	77,740	15,280	17,030	23,140	**249,720**
	+/–	–22	–24	–19	–7	–22	–26	–10	–18	**–19**
	02	16,990	14,110	41,260	23,450	60,600	11,380	15,320	19,000	**202,110**
Independent	94	3,090	1,130	4,930	7,430	21,170	2,130	3,600	4,540	**48,020**
	+/–	+2	+18	–21	–2	–8	–6	–6	+1	**–6**
	94	3,160	1,330	3,880	7,290	19,380	2,000	3,380	4,590	**45,010**
Smaller Denoms.	94	3,390	2,100	2,970	3,110	13,700	2,220	1,570	2,960	**32,020**
	+/–	+4	+7	–19	–4	–19	–10	+7	–10	**–11**
	02	3,510	2,240	2,410	2,980	11,160	2,000	1,680	2,660	**28,640**
Baptist	94	2,550	1,330	1,000	4,280	11,740	1,670	790	1,170	**24,530**
	+/–	+16	–8	–15	+21	–5	–2	–11	+1	**+1**
	02	2,950	1,230	850	5,170	11,110	1,640	700	1,180	**24,830**
Other Presbyterian	94	1,410	260	1,770	2,080	5,730	430	1,590	10,040	**23,310**
	+/–	+5	–27	–34	+12	–1	–5	+2	–7	**–5**
	02	1,480	190	1,170	2,320	5,680	410	1,620	9,300	**22,170**
Episcopal	94	3,020	550	810	3,930	5,680	630	1,900	3,830	**20,350**
	+/–	+9	–53	–46	–7	–4	–8	–15	–6	**–7**
	02	3,290	260	440	3,650	5,440	580	1,620	3,590	**18,870**
Total All Scotland	94	46,330	38,340	84,150	98,530	228,940	29,220	68,860	96,750	**691,120**
	+/–	–15	–26	–24	–8	–19	–22	–16	–15	**–18**
	02	39,610	28,200	63,750	90,500	184,510	22,800	58,080	82,680	**570,130**

While the Catholics and Church of Scotland have a strong presence in City Centres, most other denominations are there also. The Catholics are stronger than the Church of Scotland in Urban Priority Areas, New Towns, and, especially, in Housing Schemes, but the Church of Scotland is stronger in Suburban areas and Rural Areas, both Dormitory and Other. The Independents, Smaller Denominations and Baptists are all particularly strong in Towns, the Other Presbyterians in Other, remoter, Rural Areas. The Scottish Episcopal Church has the highest percentage in City Centres, owing to a number of very large churches, a number of them Cathedrals, in such.

However the interest in Table 5.8 is less the strengths and weaknesses of different denominations, but the fact, that *all five* of the other denominational groups *grew* in the City Centres between 1994 and 2002. Two saw growth in Urban Priority Areas, and a different two saw growth in Suburban areas, and two in both Dormitory Rural and Other Rural Areas. There was no growth by any denomination, however, in Housing Schemes, Towns or New Towns.

The overall growth in the City Centres across the five lesser denominations is from a total of 13,460 people in 1994 to 14,390 by 2002, an overall growth of 7%. Although two new churches were started in this period (both in the Smaller Denominations group), the average congregation has increased from 122 in 1994 to 128 by 2002, which may not be a vast increase, but in the context of a report which is mostly looking at declining congregations, this is something to be noted.

Environment by age-group

How does environment vary with age? Table 5.9 gives the basic numbers for 2002 by environment, and Figure 5.10 shows the proportion in each age-group. Similar information for 1994 has not been published.

Table 5.9: Sunday church attendance by age-group and environment, 2002

Environment	Under 15	15–19	20–29	30–44	45–64	65/65+	Total	Avge Age
City Centre	6,930	1,740	2,880	6,040	10,830	11,190	**39,610**	46
Urban Priority Area	4,920	1,230	1,900	4,220	7,800	8,130	**28,200**	46
Housing Scheme	11,400	2,920	4,350	9,820	17,690	17,570	**63,750**	45
Suburban	15,350	3,580	5,590	12,350	24,920	28,710	**90,500**	47
Town	31,920	7,750	12,290	26,380	50,520	55,650	**184,510**	47
New Town	4,040	1,030	1,660	3,520	6,240	6,310	**22,800**	45
Rural: Dormitory	9,740	2,210	3,280	7,630	16,110	19,110	**58,080**	48
Rural: Other Area	14,120	3,340	4,760	10,860	22,530	27,070	**82,680**	48
Total All Scotland	**98,420**	**23,800**	**36,710**	**80,820**	**156,640**	**173,740**	570,130	47

Figure 5.10: Proportions attending church by age and environment, 2002

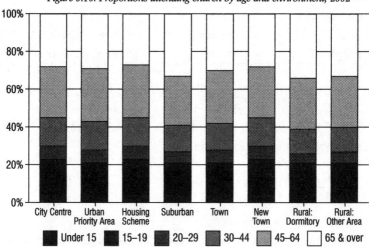

It is immediately obvious from the diagram that there are very small variations in age across the different church environments. Whatever makes churches grow in different locations it is not primarily a response to the age of the congregation. There are slightly younger people in church in Housing Schemes and slightly older people in church in rural areas, but these are hardly dramatic findings, and are, after all, what might have been expected!

Average congregational size

Finally in this chapter, we look briefly at the average size of a congregation, broken down by 3 of the different factors available, which is given in the following Table:

Table 5.11: Average size of a congregation by different factors, 2002

Denomination	Av. size	Churchmanship	Av. size	Environment	Av. size
Church of Scotland	140	Broad	110	City Centre	220
Roman Catholic	340	Catholic	300	Urban Priority Areas	130
Independent	80	Evan: Charismatic	100	Housing Scheme	170
Smaller denominations	60	Evan: Mainstream	120	Suburban	230
Baptist	120	Evan: Reformed	90	Town	165
Other Presbyterian	65	Liberal	110	New Town	200
Episcopal	60	Low Church	100	Rural: Dormitory	125
All Scotland	**140**	Reformed	130	Rural: Other Area	65

The largest congregations are the Roman Catholic, followed by Catholic, Suburban and City Centre churches. The smallest are those in the Scottish Episcopal Church, Other Presbyterian churches and remoter Other Rural areas.

So what does all this say?

In this chapter we have seen:
- Only the Mainstream Evangelical churchmanship wing of the churches in Scotland grew between 1994 and 2002, the same as in England.
- Trends against the overall pattern were an increasing number of Liberals in the Scottish Episcopal Church and a small increase in Evangelicals in the Roman Catholic Church, which otherwise dropped in attendance in all other areas of churchmanship.
- The Mainstream Evangelical growth came mostly through the Church of Scotland, Independent and Other Presbyterian churches.

- Churchmanship and denomination are often closely related, with proportions changing little between 1994 and 2002.
- Charismatics have by far the youngest age profile, and Broad, Liberal, Low Church and Reformed by far the oldest.
- While a third of Scottish churchgoers attend churches in towns, it is the suburban churches, to which a sixth go, which have decreased least in the eight years to 2002.
- As with churchmanship, there is a relationship between environment and denomination.
- Apart from the Church of Scotland and Roman Catholic Church, the other denominations all saw growth in their City Centre congregations during the second half of the 1990s.
- The age of people going to church does not vary greatly by environment – Housing Schemes have slightly younger congregations on average, and Rural Areas older.
- The largest congregations on average are Roman Catholic, Catholic, Suburban and City Centre in that order, and the smallest are Episcopal, Other Presbyterian and remoter Rural Areas.

NOTES

[1] A detailed description of how these were derived is given in *Religious Trends,* No 3.

[2] See Tables 12.30–36.4.

[3] *Prospects for Scotland 2000,* Peter Brierley and Fergus MacDonald, Christian Research, London, and National Bible Society for Scotland, Edinburgh, 1995, Pages 229–245.

6) Church growth

When it is known that the results of another church census are on the way, the assumption often seems to be that the picture will be downhill all the way. That is not true! It is no more true in Scotland than elsewhere! Even when the overall results are one of decline, it should never be assumed that every church is declining.

It is possible to compare the answers given by churches in 2002 with those they gave to the Scottish Church Census in 1994, for those churches which completed both forms. Of the 2,147 forms completed for the 2002 Census, just over a third, 36%, or 772, came from churches which had also completed forms in 1994. This third is equivalent to one-fifth, 19%, of all the churches, 4,144, in Scotland in 2002[1].

This is a sufficient size sample to use this information for a number of comparisons. It is possible to determine very easily exactly how much these churches grew or declined:

- 6% grew more than 60% between 1994 and 2002
- 15% grew between 10% and 59%
- 15% remained stable, changing between +9% and –9%
- 14% declined between –10% and –24%
- 14% declined between –25% and –39%
- 18% declined between –40% and –59%, and
- 18% declined –60% or more.

Thus in these 8 years, 21% of Scottish churches (extrapolating this sample to all the churches) grew, 15% remained stable, and two-thirds, 64%, declined. The cumulative effect of the declining congregations swallowed up the growth of the increasing congregations.

These percentages are almost identical to those in England for the period 1989 to 1998, when they were, respectively, 22%, 14% and 64%.

Could some of the decline simply be because some congregational members transferred to growing churches? Yes, it could, but unfortunately no direct measurement of this is possible from the data collected in the Census. Studies in England suggest that up to two-thirds of those joining growing churches are transfers from other churches, but it is not known whether this percentage would apply in Scotland.

Comparative figures

Figure 6.1 shows how the Scottish percentages of growing and declining churches have varied since 1980[2]. Unfortunately, the earlier figures were calculated on a much stricter formula of whether a church had grown 20% over a four year period (with a congregation of 50 or more) or 100% with a smaller congregation. They do not therefore directly compare with the most recent period when if a church grew at least 10% over eight years it has been counted as a growing church[3].

If the earlier formula was used over the most recent period, it would appear that only about 6% of churches would count as growing, and 50% would be counted as stable, with 44% declining.

Figure 6.1: Growing and declining churches since 1980

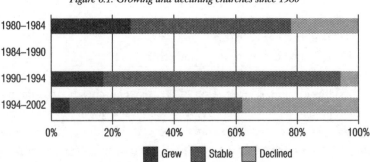

For ease of comparison these three percentages have been used in Figure 6.1, but not elsewhere in this chapter.

On this basis, it may be seen that the number of stable churches has diminished, the number of declining congregations has greatly increased, and the proportion of growing churches shrunk considerably. If it is true (as Figure 6.1 might suggest) that the stable congregations of yesterday become the declining congregations of today, then with so many stable churches today the future for Scottish congregations is sombre. But, on the other hand, why can't the stable churches of today become the growing congregations of tomorrow?

A similar analysis for English congregations between 1989 and 1998 found that 21% had grown (of which 7% more than 60%), 14% were stable and 65% declined[4]. Thus Scotland has a smaller proportion of churches which grew, and fewer which were stable, and more which declined.

Growth and decline by size of church

How much did the percentage of churches which grew and declined vary by the size of their congregation? Table 6.2 answers for 2002 and Table 6.3 for 1994. Statistically, the figures in Table 6.2 are significant[5]. There is a correlation between size of church and declining congregations. Nearly two-fifths, 36%, of churches with current congregations of under 50 have declined at least 60% in the 8 years 1994 to 2002.

It should however also be noted that almost two-fifths, 39%, of the largest churches (over 200) have seen decline between 10% and 39% in the same period, but that a third, 31%, of them have grown, a much higher percentage than for any other size church. A quarter, 24%, of churches with congregations between 101 and 200 have dropped between 40% and 59% in this eight year period.

The average size of churches, given in the bottom line, shows that (apart from "macro" growing churches) the smaller the church

the greater the likelihood of it being a declining congregation. The
"macro" growth churches are mostly new churches, started in the
last ten years.

Table 6.2: Growth and decline by size of congregation, 2002

Size in 2002	Macro growth (+60% & over) %	Micro growth (+10% ...59%) %	Stable (+9% ...−9%) %	Micro decline (−10% ...−24%) %	Midi decline (−25% ...−39%) %	Medium decline (−40% ...−59%) %	Macro decline (−60% & over) %	Base
Under 50	5	10	12	10	9	18	36	321
50–100	7	18	15	15	17	18	10	191
101–200	7	14	18	15	18	24	4	163
Over 200	7	24	16	21	18	10	2	97
Overall	6	15	15	14	14	18	18	772
Average size	75	210	175	190	185	170	70	140

Table 6.3: Growth and decline by size of congregation, 1994

Size in 1994	Macro growth (+60% & over) %	Micro growth (+10% ...59%) %	Stable (+9% ...−9%) %	Micro decline (−10% ...−24%) %	Midi decline (−25% ...−39%) %	Medium decline (−40% ...−59%) %	Macro decline (−60% & over) %	Base
Under 50	14	19	16	14	10	12	15	216
50–100	7	16	15	12	10	14	26	182
101–200	2	14	16	15	16	22	15	187
Over 200	1	10	12	13	22	26	16	187
Overall	6	15	15	14	14	18	18	772
Average size	35	155	175	170	235	290	215	165

Table 6.3 gives the size of churches in 1994 broken down by
how they have changed in the following eight years. Thus, for
example, 14% of churches whose congregations were under 50
in 1994 saw growth in excess of 60%. So a church of say 40 people
with a growth of exactly 60% would be 64 strong in 2002 and would
therefore be in the "50 to 100" row in Table 6.2.

Table 6.3 shows that there was a considerable proportion of churches, 40%, in the 50 to 100 category in 1994 which then declined by 60% or more, and which therefore now fall into the 36% of small churches (in Table 6.2). Almost, 48%, of the largest churches in 1994 experienced 25 to 59% decline between 1994 and 2002.

The average size of churches in each category in Table 6.3 gives a different message from that of Table 6.2. This is because many of the largest churches, in the "over 200" category, are Catholic, and many of these churches have seen decline in the period since 1994. The presence of many large churches in 1994 makes the average figures obviously larger. But Table 6.3 is similar to Table 6.2 for the "macro" growing churches, which have the smallest congregations, and for the "macro" declining churches which are, on average, smaller than those which declined between 40 and 59% between 1994 and 2002.

The figures in Table 6.3 are also statistically significant[6] showing that growth and decline is related to past size of congregation as well as present size. The relationship is actually stronger with past size than present size.

Growth and decline by Council

Figures 6.4 and 6.5 respectively show which parts of Scotland have the highest percentages of growing and declining churches, where "growing" is taken as congregations increasing at least 10% in the period 1994 and 2002 and "declining" as decreasing by at least 40%.

The highest concentrations of growing churches are in Aberdeenshire, the Scottish Borders, Stirling and Clackmannanshire and the Shetland Islands.

The highest concentrations of declining congregations are in Aberdeen City, Angus, East Dunbartonshire, Dundee City, Glasgow City, Moray, and the Western Isles (Eilean Siar), Skye and Lochalsh.

Figures 6.4 and 6.5 do not compare well with the maps in Chapter 3 largely because the maps in this Chapter look at growing

*Figure 6.4: Percentage of congregations which grew
more than 10% between 1994 and 2002*

☐ Under 10% ▨ 10%–14% ■ 15%–19% ■ 20% & over

churches (that is, the basic unit) not at total attendance (the basic
market). In attendance terms the amount of decline outweighs the
growth, but Figure 6.4 looks at the percentage of growing units, not
the cumulative size of those units.

Figure 6.5: Percentage of congregations which declined
more than 40% between 1994 and 2002

Under 30%   30%–39%   40%–49%   50% & over

Growth and decline by denomination

How much does congregational growth and decline vary with a
church's denomination? Table 6.6 overleaf gives the detail. There
were too few Catholic churches in this particular sample to justify
separate identification.

Table 6.6: Growth and decline by denomination, 2002

Denomination	Macro growth (+60% & over) %	Micro growth (+10% ...59%) %	Stable (+9% ...–9%) %	Micro decline (–10% ...–24%) %	Midi decline (–25% ...–39%) %	Medium decline (–40% ...–59%) %	Macro decline (–60% & over) %	Base
C. of Scotland	6	10	16	17	17	22	12	305
Independent	12	16	13	12	10	14	23	113
Smaller denms.	5	17	9	13	9	17	30	98
Baptist	6	19	18	11	14	15	17	100
Other Prsbytrn	3	19	7	12	13	18	28	90
Episcopal	5	25	25	8	15	16	6	60
Overall	6	15	15	14	14	18	18	772

These results yet again are statistically significant[7], which means that denomination is important in relation to a church's growth or decline. Over a quarter, 28%, of Independent churches saw growth, and almost a third, 30%, of Episcopal churches, but because almost a quarter, 23%, of Independent churches saw macro decline, and a quarter, 25%, of Episcopal churches remained stable, the overall position for these two denominations was lack of growth.

The overall growth in the Baptist denomination can be seen to come from a relatively small percentage, 25%, of churches which experienced growth between 1994 and 2002, the totality of which was just greater than the decline experienced by 57% of Baptist churches.

The Church of Scotland had fewer churches than average in a macro decline position but more which declined between 40 and 59%. The Smaller Denominations had fewer which were stable and nearly a third, 30%, in macro decline. The Baptists (which overall grew slightly as a denomination) had an average proportion of churches seeing macro growth but an above average proportion of churches with micro growth, between 10 and 59%. Other Presbyterian churches likewise had an above average proportion of churches seeing micro growth, but had over a quarter, 28%, of churches experiencing macro decline which more than offset the growth.

Although growth and decline often vary by churchmanship, it was not possible to measure this accurately in this census due to there being too many Evangelical churches amongst those which had completed forms in both 1994 and 2002[8]. However we can analyse the figures by environment.

Growth and decline by environment

How much does congregational growth and decline relate to a church's immediate environment? Table 6.7 gives the detail; some categories are grouped together because the individual numbers were too small to use reliably by themselves. The figures incidentally show that a third of the churches which replied to both surveys were in rural areas. As overall only a quarter of churches are in such areas, it means that rural churches were especially good at replying!

Table 6.7: Growth and decline by environment, 2002

Environment	Macro growth (+60% & over) %	Micro growth (+10% ...59%) %	Stable (+9% ...−9%) %	Micro decline (−10% ...−24%) %	Midi decline (−25% ...−39%) %	Medium decline (−40% ...−59%) %	Macro decline (−60% & over) %	Base
CC/UPA/HS	9	10	9	17	13	21	21	141
Suburban	2	12	17	11	21	26	11	98
Town/New town	5	17	18	14	15	14	17	264
Rural (D&O)	8	17	14	14	11	17	19	250
Overall	6	15	15	14	14	18	18	772

CC/UPA/HS: City Centre/Urban Priority Area/Housing Scheme
Rural (D&O): Rural (Dormitory & Other)

These results are again statistically significant[9], which means that environment does play a part in a church's growth or decline. The greatest variation is for churches in suburban locations, which were much more likely to see significant decline (between 25% and 59%) but not macro decline of 60% or more. Churches in City

Centres, Urban Priority Areas or Housing Scheme were less likely to
have remained stable, and as Table 5.8 indicated, to have declined if
Church of Scotland or Roman Catholic, but grown if in the other
denominations.

Growth and decline by age of congregation

Does the age distribution of a congregation impact whether it is
growing or declining? The answer is NO[10], although Table 6.8 shows
certain trends[11]:

- The percentage of people 65 and over gradually increases as you
  move from left to right, although it goes down in the final, macro
  decline, column. This indicates higher proportions of older people
  in declining congregations.
- Conversely, although to a more limited extent, the percentage of
  people aged 30 to 44 reduces across the Table. Growing congregations have a higher percentage of people in this age-group than
  declining congregations. This is a key age-group, supplying not
  only children (!) but also leadership to many church activities.

Table 6.8: Age distribution within growing and declining churches, 2002

Age-group	Macro growth (+60% & over) %	Micro growth (+10% ...59%) %	Stable (+9% ...–9%) %	Micro decline (–10% ...–24%) %	Midi decline (–25% ...–39%) %	Medium decline (–40% ...–59%) %	Macro decline (–60% & over) %	Over -all
Under 12	12	13	14	14	13	12	12	13
12 to 14	4	7	4	4	4	3	4	4
15 to 19	6	5	5	4	2	3	4	4
20 to 29	5	7	6	7	5	5	6	6
30 to 44	15	15	15	15	13	13	12	14
45 to 64	34	26	28	27	26	27	30	28
65 and over	24	27	28	29	37	37	32	31
Base	32	73	78	104	142	171	172	772
Average age	46	45	46	46	50	50	48	47

- The percentage of people under 30 also broadly reduces as you go from growth to decline (being, respectively, 27%, 32%, 29%, 29%, 24%, 23% and 26%), indicating churches with micro growth have the highest proportion of younger people.
- All the above is summed up in the final row of the Table which gives the average age. Congregations which have declined between 25 and 59% have the highest average age, and those which have experienced micro growth the lowest.

However, unlike the other characteristics which have been examined, the differences in age-groups (taken as a group) across growth and decline are not statistically significant.

Growth and decline by financial change over the previous year

Did a growing congregation correlate with growing finance over the past year? Table 6.9 indicates the answer is YES, and this is statistically significant[12]. The top line goes down steadily as you move across the Table.

Table 6.9: Growth and decline by financial change over the previous year

Over the past year, finances...	Macro growth (+60% & over) %	Micro growth (+10% ...59%) %	Stable (+9% ...–9%) %	Micro decline (–10% ...–24%) %	Midi decline (–25% ...–39%) %	Medium decline (–40% ...–59%) %	Macro decline (–60% & over) %	Over -all
Grew	77	71	70	68	66	54	52	62
Were stable	15	27	26	29	27	35	35	30
Declined	8	2	4	3	7	11	13	8
Base	32	68	74	102	136	162	160	734

Growth and decline by expectation of growth and decline

Did a growing congregation say they expected to grow yet more by 2010? Table 6.10 gives the answer, which again is YES, and this also is statistically significant[13]. The top line again decreases steadily as you move across the Table.

Table 6.10: Growth and decline by expectation of growth and decline

By 2010, we expect this church to have...	Macro growth (+60% & over) %	Micro growth (+10% ...59%) %	Stable (+9% ...–9%) %	Micro decline (–10% ...–24%) %	Midi decline (–25% ...–39%) %	Medium decline (–40% ...–59%) %	Macro decline (–60% & over) %	Over -all %
Grown signif.	36	31	23	22	16	16	16	20
Grown little	16	40	42	38	43	33	35	37
Remain stable	39	12	22	25	26	22	17	22
Declined	9	17	13	12	13	28	28	19
Closed	0	0	0	3	2	1	4	2
Base	30	65	77	100	133	156	156	717

Growth and decline by previous growth and decline

The 1994 Census asked for attendances four years previously in 1990. It was therefore possible to calculate which congregations had grown or declined between 1990 and 1994, though the previous report only gave the figures using adult attendance, so the comparison is not completely one-to-one. Did a congregation growing or declining between 1994 and 2002 correlate with their previous experience? Table 6.11 indicates the answer is NO; the figures are not significant.

Table 6.11: Growth and decline by adult growth and decline, 1990–1994

Between 1990–1994 the number of adults in our church...	Macro growth (+60% & over) %	Micro growth (+10% ...59%) %	Stable (+9% ...–9%) %	Micro decline (–10% ...–24%) %	Midi decline (–25% ...–39%) %	Medium decline (–40% ...–59%) %	Macro decline (–60% & over) %	Over -all %
Grew	21	9	17	19	18	13	21	17
Remain stable	76	83	74	71	81	81	73	77
Declined	3	8	9	10	1	6	6	6
Base	29	67	78	99	135	159	163	730

Growth and decline by holding of midweek or youth services

Did churches holding midweek and/or youth services vary in terms of growth or decline? The answer was NO for midweek services but YES to youth services, a combination also found in England, although the direction was different. The results are given in Table 6.12, with Youth Services being statistically significant[14].

Table 6.12: Growth and decline by midweek and youth services, 2002

YES, hold services	Macro growth (+60% & over) %	Micro growth (+10% ...59%) %	Stable (+9% ...–9%) %	Micro decline (–10% ...–24%) %	Midi decline (–25% ...–39%) %	Medium decline (–40% ...–59%) %	Macro decline (–60% & over) %	Over -all %
Midweek	51	60	56	48	59	54	60	56
For youth	36	46	44	50	56	50	39	47
Base	32	73	78	104	142	171	172	772

While it is true that holding Youth Services is a contributing feature to growth or decline, the Scottish finding is the reverse of that found in England. In England, holding youth services was associated with growing churches; in Scotland they are more likely to be associated with declining churches! But we have already seen that children and youth church attendance in Scotland is different from that south of the border (Scotland is losing parents rather than children while England is losing parents as well as children), so the finding about youth services is perhaps part of the attempt of Scottish churches to halt the exodus of children with their parents.

One third, 33%, of churches held other events at which adults came to the church during the week but who did not attend on Sunday, and 20% activities for children. Neither varied by growth or decline. 57% of churches had members of their congregation involved in community service. This did not vary significantly with growth or decline, although churches which grew had 63% of members involved, and churches which had declined at least 40% had only 52%.

Growth and decline by holding Alpha courses

Was growth or decline in congregations associated with whether churches had held an Alpha or Emmaus course? The answer was NO statistically for Alpha courses[15], with Table 6.13 providing the details. Too few churches had held an Emmaus course for any comparative figures to be reliable; the percentages are given in Table 6.13, and if anything show that Emmaus courses tend to be held most by declining churches!

Table 6.13: Growth and decline by holding Alpha and Emmaus courses

YES, we have held courses called...	Macro growth (+60% & over) %	Micro growth (+10% ...59%) %	Stable (+9% ...–9%) %	Micro decline (–10% ...–24%) %	Midi decline (–25% ...–39%) %	Medium decline (–40% ...–59%) %	Macro decline (–60% & over) %	Over -all
Alpha	31	32	25	35	26	28	20	27
Emmaus	0	1.7	0	0	4	1	1.3	1.3
Base	32	73	78	104	142	171	172	772

A third, 33%, of growing churches had held an Alpha course, but only a quarter, 24%, of churches which had declined 40% or more. Interestingly, just over a third, 35%, of churches which had declined between 10 and 14% had also held an Alpha course, presumably to see if they could reverse their downward trend.

Growing churches had held more Alpha courses than declining churches – churches which had grown had held 4.1 Alpha courses to 3.3 courses by churches which had declined at least 40%. Curiously, churches which had declined between 25 and 39% had held an average of 4.9 Alpha courses. In England both the holding of Alpha courses and their frequency was significant; perhaps Alpha has not been used in Scottish churches as long, or perhaps publicity has been less effective in less densely populated areas. The numbers attending Alpha courses did not vary by whether a church was growing or declining[16].

Growth and decline by number of lay leaders

Was growth or decline associated with the number of lay leaders that a church had? The answer was YES, and the results were significant[17]. The number of forms in this sample from Catholic churches was too few to give reliable results for Catholic Lay Ministries, so the focus is only here on the Elders, Deacons, etc. of Protestant denominations. Do growing churches have more or fewer leaders? Table 6.14 gives the answer:

Table 6.14: Protestant growth and decline by number of lay leaders

Number of lay leaders	Macro growth (+60% and over) %	Micro growth (+10% ...59%) %	Stable (+9% ...–9%) %	Micro decline (–10% ...–24%) %	Midi decline (–25% ...–39%) %	Medium decline (–40% ...–59%) %	Macro decline (–60% and over) %	Over -all
1–10	64	61	41	46	40	42	74	52
11–20	18	24	25	20	16	22	11	19
21–30	4	3	11	7	9	9	6	7
31–50	14	7	16	15	16	15	6	12
Over 50	0	5	7	12	19	12	3	10
Base	28	59	61	85	116	136	143	628
Average no.	13	13	19	20	25	21	11	8

Growing churches have a smaller leadership team. As you move across Table 6.14 from left to right the average number of lay leaders (bottom line) increases rising to a peak of 25 for churches which experienced decline of between 25 and 39%. Churches experiencing greater decline had fewer leaders, but almost certainly because they had great difficulty in finding enough leaders. This was especially true of the churches which have declined most rapidly; those able to lead, realising that their church was in a weak position, may perhaps have left for another church.

As four-fifths, 80%, of all Scottish lay leaders in the Protestant churches are in the Church of Scotland[18], this strongly points to the desirability of reducing the number of Elders in these churches. Perhaps one of the reasons why the Church of Scotland has declined is because there are too many Elders. Appointed for life, many of these older people, who are more likely to resist change, and thus hold back their churches from progressing to new activities, thereby limiting the opportunity to grow.

So many factors!

This chapter has deliberately sought from the questions asked in either the 1994 or the 2002 Scottish Church Censuses, to try and find what causes churches to grow. The analysis has been limited by the questions actually asked in those surveys. Other, probably more important, questions, such as the vision and gifting of the leader, quality of the worship or warmth of welcome (all of which are relevant in the English scene), cannot be answered from the statistical analysis. They were, however, shown to be important in the Focus Groups (see Chapter 10).

We can however summarise the findings, and the final Table of this chapter does this:

Table 6.15: Factors for growth or decline or neither

Factors associated with growth	Factors associated with decline	Factors which were neutral
Congregations over 200 in 2002	Congregations over 50 in 1994	Growth or decline between 1990 and 1994
Located in western areas or the Shetland Isles	Located in cities* or the Western Isles	Holding midweek services
Being Independent or Episcopal	Being Church of Scotland or a smaller denomination	Frequency of Alpha or numbers attending
Expecting to grow	Churches in suburban areas	
Increasing finance	Holding youth services	
Having fewer lay leaders	Holding Emmaus courses	

If Church of Scotland or Roman Catholic

The question is bound to be asked, "Which, of all these factors, are the most important for growth?" The answer is two-fold: The expectation of growth (which might perhaps be translated as "having a vision of what the church could become") and having a small number of lay leaders. Both these factors revolve around the issue of LEADERSHIP. As the Focus Groups and other studies have also shown, this is the key issue.

Which of these factors was most associated with decline? Again the answer is two-fold: The size of the congregation in 1994, and the location of the church, both factors which cannot be changed. However, it should be noted that opposite factors, such as size of congregation in 2002 or other locations are not necessarily the key significant factors for growth. Growth and decline are associated with different elements, the reverse of which does not always seem to apply.

NOTES

[1] In a similar English analysis, the number of churches which responded in both 1989 and 1998, was equivalent also to a fifth, 22%, of all the 37,700 churches in England.

[2] The proportions of churches which grew and declined were not calculated between 1984 and 1990, and it is not now possible to do so.

[3] The more detailed evaluation of growth and decline allows more sophisticated analyses to be undertaken.

[4] *Church Growth in the 1990s,* Peter Brierley, Springboard, Abingdon and Christian Research, London, March 2000.

[5] For those wanting the actual statistical figures, $P = 0.002^*$, $r = -0.052$, $t = -2.40^*$, where * indicates significance below 5% (and ** below 0.1%).

[6] $P < 0.001^{**}$, $r = +0.922$, $t = 110.45^{**}$.

[7] $P < 0.001^{**}$, $r = -0.068$, $t = -3.16^*$.

[8] Congregational growth and decline depended to a very small extent on their churchmanship in England. However, a disproportionate number of Scotland's Evangelical churches replied, and removing the two-thirds of these necessary to give the correct proportion would reduce the whole sample size of churches replying in 1994 and 2002 to be too small for viable analysis. In addition some churches which indicated they were "evangelical" in 1994 gave a different churchmanship in 2002, and vice versa, so reliable figures for growth and decline by churchmanship consistent with the other figures which have emerged from the Census are unfortunately unobtainable.

[9] $P < 0.001^{**}$, $r = +0.881$, $t = 86.4^{**}$.

[10] $X^2 = 30.6$, df $= 36$, $P = 0.721$.

[11] It should be noted that the number on which the macro growth column is estimated is extremely small and the percentages in it will have relatively large margins of error – for example the 34% is within the range of 18 to 50%.

[12] $P = 0.001^*$, $r = -0.009$, $t = -0.39$.

[13] $P < 0.001^{**}$, $r = -0.120$, $t = -5.26^{**}$.

[14] $X^2 = 20.2$, df $= 6$, $P = 0.0025^*$.

[15] $t = 1.36$, df $= 6$, $P = 0.118$.

[16] $X^2 = 34.3$, df $= 30$, $P = 0.270$.

[17] $X^2 = 67.1$, df $= 24$, $P < 0.001^{**}$.

[18] See Table 9.1.

7) Midweek activities

Thus far, we have concentrated on Sunday church attendance. However, many people are involved with church midweek either as well as on Sunday or instead of on Sunday. The Census form asked three broad questions about the range of midweek activities that churches undertake: worship services, youth activities and midweek activities attended by people who do not come on Sundays.

Midweek worship

The first of these questions asked "Do you have regular midweek worship (eg services, cell groups, etc.)?" Just over half, 56%, of churches answered YES to this question, which compares with 42% in England. This varied considerably by denomination as Figure 7.1 illustrates.

Figure 7.1: Churches with midweek worship, 2002

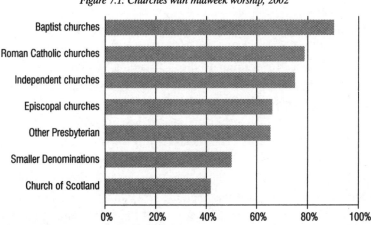

Average attendance at these services was 27 people (in England it was 21), and this also varied by denomination. It went from:

- 49 for Catholic churches
- 33 for Baptist
- 25 for Independent
- 24 for Episcopal, Other Presbyterian, and Smaller Denominations, to
- 20 for Church of Scotland churches.

On the assumption that the churches which did not reply held midweek worship as frequently and with as many people coming on average, then overall this comes to a total of 69,300 people going to midweek worship, or 1.4% of the population. In England the total number coming was half this at 0.7% of the population, but given that Sunday attendance in England is two-thirds what it is in Scotland, the Scottish percentage could be expected to be higher, say, expected to be 1.0%. If the assumption that other churches had as many midweek services with so many coming is incorrect, then the 1.4% will be too high; suppose it is arbitrarily taken as midway between 1.0% and 1.4%, then it would be 1.2%.

In England it was further assumed that three-quarters of those attending midweek did not attend on Sunday, an assumption which is perhaps less true in Scotland given the higher churchgoing. Suppose only half attending midweek do not come on Sunday, then this would mean that 0.6% of the population are attending midweek worship services in addition to those attending Sunday services. Put another way, this would mean that for every 20 people coming to church on Sunday one was coming to a church service midweek and not on Sunday. Total worship attendance in Scotland is therefore 5% higher if midweek attendance is taken into consideration.

Just under two-fifths, 38%, of midweek worshippers are men, and 62% women. This is slightly less than the 40% of Sunday attenders, and would suggest that men are less likely to attend midweek perhaps because more of them are in full-time employment.

On the assumption that children do not attend midweek worship, then Figure 7.2 compares the age profile of midweek attenders with adults worshipping on Sunday. It shows that there are slightly more worshipping midweek under 20 and 45 or over and rather fewer aged 20 to 44. There is no gender difference for those under 20 or aged 45 to 64, but slightly more men attend midweek than women aged 20 to 44 (23% to 19%) and slightly more women than men who are 65 or over (41% to 38%).

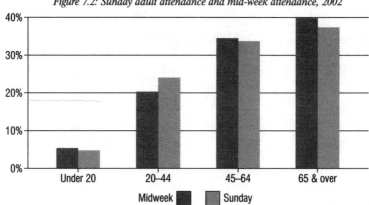

Figure 7.2: Sunday adult attendance and mid-week attendance, 2002

On how many days did church have midweek worship? 56% (of those which have such a service at all) had it on one day only, 15% on two days, 15% on 3 days, 2% on 4 days, 10% on 5 days and 2% every day. One in seven, 15%, held it on Mondays, 19% on Tuesdays, 30% on Wednesday (the most popular day), 23% on Thursday, 11% on Friday and 2% on a Saturday.

For just over half, 51%, of the churches the most usual time for starting their midweek service was at 7.00 pm in the evening, followed by a fifth, 20%, which preferred 10.00 am in the morning. No other time slot was used anything like as much: 7% of churches had a service in the 9.00 am hour, 6% in the 8.00 pm hour. 2% had a service before 9.00 am, 5% between 11.00 am and 1.00 pm, and 9% had a service in the afternoon or early evening between 1.00 and 7.00 pm.

Youth activities

Did churches hold regular youth activities during the week such as
Boys' Brigade, Brownies, Youth Club, etc? Almost half, 47%, of
churches said YES, they did. This varied with denomination, as
shown in Figure 7.3:

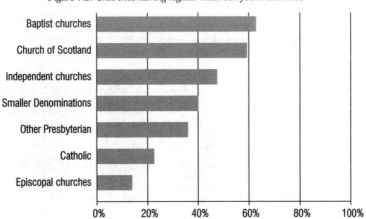

Figure 7.3: Churches having regular midweek youth activities

The average number of young people at these activities is 59, but this
figure is distorted by a large Church of Scotland figure of 70 per
church, and the average of all the other churches combined is just
over half this size, 38 per church. Huge emphasis is placed on midweek activities by the Church of Scotland, and this success shows
through in these basic numbers. The other denominations had average attendances of:
• 52 for Baptist churches
• 37 for Independent churches
• 36 for Smaller Denominations
• 35 for Roman Catholics
• 31 for Episcopal churches
• 30 for Other Presbyterian churches.

This size order is quite different from the numbers attending midweek worship services, and reflects different traditions, theologies and priorities between the denominations.

The number of young people involved in these youth activities is quite high. Collectively they amount to 102,000 young people, two-thirds, 68%, of whom are Church of Scotland. This is 6.6% of the population under 25 years of age.

In gender terms the young people are more balanced, 46% boys and 54% girls, virtually the same as Sunday attendance for those under 30 (48% and 52%). Figure 7.4 compares midweek youth attendance with Sunday attendance, taking the oldest category of "youth" to be aged 20 to 24.

There were more girls 11 and under than boys (63% to 57%), but more older teenage boys than girls (11% to 7%), perhaps because they were helpers at these activities.

Figure 7.4: Midweek and Sunday attendance by young people, 2002

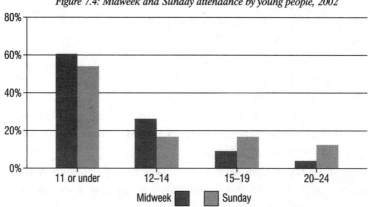

Those under 15 are more likely to come to a midweek activity than Sunday church. This result agrees with the findings of a specifically Church of Scotland study undertaken in 2001[1]. Older young people are more likely to be in church. Other research[2] reinforces this finding of the importance and popularity of midweek activities. Why are they so popular? The Church of Scotland study found the following reasons:

- Youth clubs generally are "fun" (and church isn't)!
- Youth clubs usually have food available (and church doesn't)!
- Young people can choose whether or not they wish to go to a youth club. While they invariably will go, they have the choice. When taken to church by their parents, they don't have that choice (and consequently often leave when parents eventually do give them the choice).
- Parents are not involved at youth club, so they can "be themselves", whereas in church their parents are somewhere around.

The favourite day for a youth activity was Friday, with 22% of churches holding one that day, but the other days during the week were about as popular – 18% were held on Wednesday, another 18% on Thursday, with 17% on each of Monday and Tuesday. Just 8% were held over the weekend (5% Sunday, 3% Saturday).

The most popular hour for starting youth activities was 6.00 pm (57% of churches), followed by 7.00 pm (29%). Of the remaining 14%, 2% were held in the morning, 10% earlier in the late afternoon and 2% at 8.00 pm.

Half, 49%, of churches which run such an activity had only one, but a fifth, 22%, had two, and 13% had three, with the remaining seventh, 14%, having four or more per week.

What percentage of young people usually attended Sunday services? The overall answer across Scotland is 14%, but Table 7.5 breaks this percentage down by denomination. A fifth, 20%, of Baptist young people who go to their midweek youth activities attend church on Sunday on average, against only 6% from Episcopal churches. Other denominations are between these extremes.

If only 14% of the young people attending church youth activities go to church on Sunday, that leaves 86% who are in a "faith culture" but not in church. This amounts to 5.7% of Scottish young people under 25, which in turn is equivalent to 1.7% of the population.

Table 7.5: Percentage of young people at midweek youth clubs
who attend church on Sunday

Denomination	0% %	1–24% %	25–49% %	50–74% %	75–99% %	100% %	Average %
Church of Scotland	53	29	9	5	2	2	14%
Roman Catholic	81	2	3	4	5	5	13%
Independent	63	15	5	5	7	5	18%
Smaller denoms.	74	11	3	5	2	5	12%
Baptist	47	25	10	11	4	3	20%
Other Presbyterian	70	12	9	4	4	1	12%
Episcopal	89	4	1	1	1	4	6%
Total All Scotland	63	19	7	5	3	3	14%

Other midweek activities

The final question in this "midweek" section asked churches to estimate the number of people who usually attended midweek church-
run activities, such as Drop In Centres, Mothers & Toddlers, Lunch
Clubs, etc, but who did not regularly attend worship services at the
church. Respondents were specifically asked to exclude outside
organisations who hired or made use of church premises. A third,
33%, of churches gave adult numbers who came and a fifth, 20%,
numbers of children. As before, the percentage of churches with
such midweek activities varied by denomination, as shown in Figure
7.6 for adult activities, overleaf.

The Independent churches are much more likely to be running
activities midweek for those who do not attend church regularly,
presumably because this is one of their main forms of outreach and
service to the community. Four in five Independent churches, 80%,
have such activities, against 29% collectively for churches of all
other denominations.

The average number who attend these activities is 41 adults
and 32 children under 15, a total of 73, virtually identical to the
English total of 70 made up of 37 adults and 33 children. Naturally

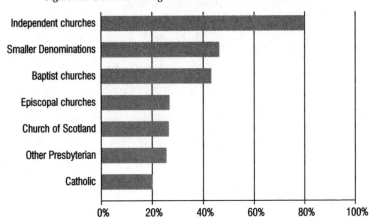

Figure 7.6: Churches having midweek church-run adult activities

this varies by denomination, as follows:
- 111: 60 adults and 51 children in Church of Scotland churches
- 96: 47 adults and 49 children in Baptist churches
- 64: 44 adults and 20 children in Roman Catholic churches
- 53: 32 adults and 21 children in Smaller Denominations
- 37: 23 adults and 14 children in Independent churches
- 27: 16 adults and 11 children in Episcopal churches
- 16: 9 adults and 7 children in Other Presbyterian churches.

The aggregate number of people involved in these activities is quite high. Collectively they amount to 52,900 adults and 26,800 children, a total of 79,700 people, 1.6% of the population (2.9% of the child population and 1.3% of the adult). By definition, these are not regular attenders on Sunday but are attending church-run events during the week – a group who are often called the "fringe". The overall English percentage is higher, 2.4%, because a higher percentage of churches are involved in such activities (45% to Scotland's 33%).

In gender terms the children are 44% male, 56% female; the adults 28% male, 72% female. Figure 7.7 shows how these compare with church attendance percentages.

Figure 7.7: Midweek fringe and Sunday church attendance, 2002

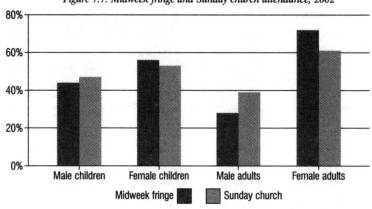

The fringe activities attract children in broadly the same proportions as Sunday church does, but they attract more adult women. Does this mean some women attend these activities rather than church?

The average numbers attending "fringe" events are much more monochrome when broken down by churchmanship. Denomination is the more important factor in this regard. The actual numbers are:

- 88: 57 adults and 31 children in Catholic churches
- 80: 51 adults and 29 children in Evangelical Charismatic churches
- 77: 46 adults and 31 children in Liberal churches
- 76: 38 adults and 38 children in Broad churches
- 70: 37 adults and 33 children in Evangelical Mainstream churches
- 66: 36 adults and 30 children in Evangelical Reformed churches
- 62: 34 adults and 28 children in Reformed churches
- 45: 17 adults and 28 children in Low Church churches

Community service

One question asked: "How many of the congregation are involved with community service/ care/ welfare groups?" 57% of churches replied indicating that at least one member of their congregation was so involved. The actual average was 22 people or one-sixth, 16%, of the average congregation of those having any at all.

This figure is however inflated because a few churches had a large number involved. It would give a more accurate feel if the "median" figure was used (the number up to which half the congregations had people involved and over which were the other half). This figure is 14, meaning that half the churches had up to 14 people in their congregation involved in community welfare and like groups, and the other half had more than 14. A quarter of churches had up to 5 people so involved, the next quarter between 5 and 14, and a further quarter had up to 25, with the remaining quarter more than 25.

These figures varied by denomination as Table 7.8 indicates:

Table 7.8: Proportion of congregations involved in community welfare groups by denomination, 2002

Denomination	Number of churches	% involved with community welfare	Average number in congregation	% of average congregation	Median (up to half with this number)
Church of Scotland	1,666	60	26	19	15
Roman Catholic	594	43	27	8	15
Independent	559	45	13	16	5
Smaller denominations	470	55	13	22	5
Baptist	204	64	11	9	5
Other Presbyterian	342	44	12	19	5
Episcopal	309	71	22	36[3]	10
Total All Scotland	4,144	57	22	16	14

Episcopal, Baptist and Church of Scotland (in that order) were most likely to have involvement through their congregations with community welfare. However in terms of numbers, Roman Catholic, Church of Scotland and Episcopal churches (in that order) had on average the largest numbers per congregation. But as a proportion of their congregational size it was the Episcopal, Smaller denominations, Church of Scotland/Other Presbyterian (in that order) which were involved. The names common to these three groups are the

Scottish Episcopal Church and the Church of Scotland, the two denominations which are most involved with community welfare groups.

If 22 people are involved per congregation, and 57% of congregations of the 4,144 churches in Scotland have community involvement, this is a total of 52,000 volunteers helping with the community throughout the country. This is equivalent to 1.0% of the entire population, no mean figure.

The figures also varied by churchmanship, however, and as these may be of interest, they are given in Table 7.9:

Table 7.9: Proportion of congregations involved in community welfare groups by churchmanship, 2002

Churchmanship	Number of churches	% involved with community welfare	Average number in congregation	% of average congregation	Median (up to half with this number)
Evan: Mainstream	684	57	15	13	6
Reformed	667	56	22	17	15
Catholic	617	51	25	8	15
Evan: Reformed	594	65	22	24	15
Broad	573	63	24	22	15
Liberal	484	64	29	27	15
Evan: Charismatic	286	61	25	25	10
Low Church	239	62	19	19	14
Total All Scotland	4,144	57	22	16	14

The Reformed Evangelical and Liberal churches have the highest proportion of their churches with someone in their congregations involved in community welfare. But it is the Liberals followed by the Catholic and Charismatic Evangelicals who actually have the largest numbers, with the Liberals and Charismatics with the highest percentages in their congregations.

So what does this say?

This chapter has shown a number of important elements about mid-week activities. The figures in brackets are the equivalent for England.
- 56% (42%) of Scottish churches have a midweek service. Average attendance was 27 (21), with the Catholics having the largest numbers.
- This could add a further 0.6% (0.5%) of the population to the worshipping community in Scotland, an extra 5% (9%) of Sunday churchgoers.
- These were more likely to be those 65 and over and less likely to be aged 20 to 44, compared with Sunday attenders. The majority, 56%, of churches had just one such service, frequently on a Wednesday at 7.00 pm.
- Almost half, 47%, of the churches held youth activities midweek, with a majority of Baptist, 63%, and Church of Scotland, 59%, doing so.
- Numbers of young people involved are high, 102,000, 6.6% of the relative population, two-thirds of whom are in Church of Scotland youth activities. There were proportionately more attending these activities under 15 than children attending church on Sunday.
- Half, 49%, of the churches with midweek youth activities had just one such. The most popular day for such to be held was a Friday at 6.00 pm.
- 86% of these young people did not attend church on Sunday, equivalent to 5.7% of those under 25, or 1.7% of the whole population.
- A third, 33% (45%), of churches had "fringe" events, church-led midweek activities attended by those who did not normally attend Sunday worship. Independent churches were particularly strong here, with 80% holding such.
- Average attendance was 73 (70) people, 41 (37) adults and 32 (33) children. These amount to 1.6% (2.4%) of the population. Midweek activities are more likely to attract women than men.

• More than half the churches, 57%, have members of their congregation involved with community service, care and welfare groups. On average it is about one-sixth of their congregation, 16%, who are so involved. This is a significant number of people with social concern.
• Episcopal and Church of Scotland congregations are most likely to be involved in such community groups. In terms of churchmanship it is the Liberals and Charismatic Evangelicals.

Thus to the 11.2% of the population who attend church on Sunday, a further 0.6% attend midweek but not on Sunday. In addition 1.7% of the population attend midweek youth activities run by the churches and another 1.6% go to other midweek church-run activities. Thus a total of 15.1% of the Scottish population interacts with the churches each week, three-quarters of them, 74%, on a Sunday, but a quarter, 26%, in midweek church activities. Put another way, for every three people in church on Sunday, there is another one attending a midweek church activity.

What is not known, as the data was not previously measured, is whether the midweek activity is stable or increasing or decreasing. In England it is increasing, and that could be true in Scotland also.

NOTES

[1] *Church of Scotland, Ministry among Young People* research report by Christian Research, London, 2001, for Parish Education Department, Church of Scotland.
[2] *Reaching and Keeping Tweenagers,* Peter Brierley, Christian Research, London, 2003.
[3] This compares with 25% found in a number of congregational surveys in Anglican churches in England from Christian Research studies.

8) Alpha and Emmaus events

Thanks to the huge advertising campaign each September since 1998, Alpha is recognised by 30% of the British population as a "religious course", according to a MORI poll carried out in October 2002. This is a very high recognition factor. The initial four week course originated in 1977 at Holy Trinity Church, Brompton, but was expanded to 15 sessions under the energetic leadership of Rev Nicky Gumbel in the mid 1990s[1].

It was offered to other churches in 1993 and since has expanded rapidly across the country, with Nicky Gumbel's book *Questions of Life*[2] a bestseller. In the late 1990s and the early years of the 21st century the Alpha course was used by thousands of churches across the world. In February 2002 it was known to have been held in 133 countries[3]. It has now been held in 140 countries. One of those countries is Scotland, so the Scottish Church Census explored the extent to which it had been used by churches[4].

The Emmaus course has been available for a shorter time, nor has it had the same level of publicity, and therefore has not had the chance to become so widely known. This course is in three parts: an initial module called *Contact* which aims at helping churches identify their contact groups, the basic course called *Nurture,* and then a further *Growth* course of four manuals containing an extensive menu of 15 follow-up courses. The whole was developed from an earlier course, *Christians for Life,* by a team of Anglican clergy in 1996. It takes its name from the concept that "people come to faith today through an accompanied journey rather than crisis, the Emmaus road journey"[5]. The Census explored how much this course had been used in Scotland as well.

Holding the Course

How many churches in Scotland had held these courses at all? 27% had held the Alpha course, including some in every denominational group, but only 1% the Emmaus course. As might be expected, this varied by denomination as shown in Table 8.1:

Table 8.1: Proportion of churches holding Alpha or Emmaus courses
by denomination, 2002

Course	Church of Scotland %	Roman Catholic %	Independent %	Smaller denominations %	Baptist %	Other Presbyterian %	Episcopal %	Overall %
Alpha	29	8	31	32	58	11	16	27
Emmaus	1.5	0.5	2	1	0	0	4	1.3

Although both courses emanated from Anglican stables, the Emmaus course has been used much more by the Scottish Episcopal Church than other denominations, whereas many other denominations have used the Alpha course more than the Episcopal churches. More than half, 58%, of Baptist churches have used Alpha, and almost a third of Church of Scotland[6], Independent and Smaller denominational churches. The Episcopal church, Other Presbyterians and Roman Catholics have used it least (in that order).

The Alpha course is much more charismatic in content than Emmaus, so usage by churches also differs by their churchmanship, as Table 8.2 indicates.

It is to be expected perhaps that two thirds, 69%, of charismatic churches would have used Alpha. It is perhaps less expected that over half the Reformed Evangelical churches, 52%, would also have used it, and only a third, 34%, of the Mainstream Evangelicals. While the Liberals and Catholics have used Alpha least, the Liberal churches have used Emmaus most, but this reflects the relatively high proportion of Liberal Episcopal churches.

Table 8.2: Proportion of churches holding Alpha or Emmaus courses
by churchmanship, 2002

Course	Broad %	Catholic %	Evangelical: Charismatic %	Evangelical: Mainstream %	Evangelical: Reformed %	Liberal %	Low Church %	Reformed %	Overall %
Alpha	23	9	69	34	52	14	35	25	27
Emmaus	2	1	0	1	1	3	0	1	1.3

A quarter of churches in Scotland using Alpha represents 1,120 churches. Over what kind of area were they spread? Does using Alpha vary by a church's environment? Table 8.3 gives the answer.

Table 8.3: Proportion of churches holding Alpha or Emmaus courses
by environment, 2002

Course	City Centre %	Urban Priority Centre %	Housing Scheme %	Suburban %	Town %	New Town %	Rural: Dormitory %	Rural: Other %	Overall %
Alpha	38	24	38	51	44	20	33	25	27
Emmaus	0	0	1	2	0.5	1.5	3	1.5	1.3

Suburban churches and churches in towns are most likely to have used the Alpha course, and suburban and rural dormitory churches Emmaus. Churches in areas which are new (New Towns), remote (Other Rural areas) or deprived (UPAs) use Alpha least – could this be because they are unable to find the costs of providing the meals or the helpers to run the courses?

Figure 8.4 on the next page shows where Alpha courses were held by Scottish Council. The most were held in Aberdeen City, East and Mid Lothian, East Dunbartonshire, Inverclyde, Renfrewshire and South Ayrshire. These do not relate to density of churchgoing, as some of these areas are where church attendance on a Sunday is at the lowest and some where it is highest. Nor does it relate to

Figure 8.4: Proportion of churches holding Alpha courses by Council

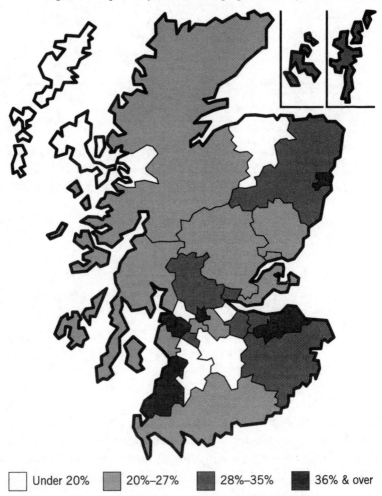

| | Under 20% | | 20%–27% | | 28%–35% | | 36% & over |

change in churchgoing, as some of these areas are seeing growth in some denominations and others seeing decline.

Although a similar map has not been drawn for the holding of Emmaus courses since so few Scottish churches have used it, if a map was drawn the places where the Emmaus course has been held most coincide almost exactly with where the Alpha courses have

been held, except for Dundee which has had relatively more
Emmaus Courses and fewer Alpha. Thus the type of course is not a
response to the area in which it is held.

Of the various factors which have been analysed, the variable
which correlates most with holding of Alpha courses is that of
churchmanship, although churches of all churchmanships have held
Alpha courses, as Table 8.2 indicates.

However it is more than likely that the key determining factor
is not type of course, denomination, churchmanship, environment or
Council, but rather the leadership of particular churches, which can,
and does, operate independently of all these factors most of the time!

Number of times course held

How many times had churches held either the Emmaus or Alpha
courses, assuming they had held it at least once? Overall the answer
is 2.3 and 3.7 times respectively. Table 8.5 breaks the answers down
by denomination.

Table 8.5: Number of times courses held, by denomination, 2002

Course	Church of Scotland %	Roman Catholic %	Independent %	Smaller denominations %	Baptist %	Other Presbyterian %	Episcopal %	Overall %
Alpha	3.7	2.2	4.0	3.0	4.2	2.0	4.6	**3.7**
Emmaus	2.5	6	1	1	0	0	2	**2.3**

It is perhaps natural that the Episcopal churches should be the
most frequent users of Alpha courses, and substantial users of the
Emmaus course also. But Baptist and Independent churches are also
important users of Alpha, though hardly at all of Emmaus. The
Church of Scotland sits in between – an average user of both courses,
and because of its size an important market.

While the average is 3.7 times per church, the reality is that half the churches have held only one or two Alpha courses (28% just one, 23% two), and the other half of the churches have held more than two. Of this other half, 23% have held three or four, which means 26% have held more than four courses. In a detailed analysis of growing churches in England, it was found that churches persevering with Alpha courses for over three years were significantly more likely to grow[7].

How long have courses been held?

Over how many years have the courses been used? One Church of Scotland church reckoned it was 20 years! The average was 3 years; this is broken down by denomination in Table 8.6.

Table 8.6: Number of years over which courses have been held, by denomination, 2002

Course	Church of Scotland %	Roman Catholic %	Independent %	Smaller denominations %	Baptist %	Other Presbyterian %	Episcopal %	Overall %
Alpha	2.9	2.1	3.2	2.7	3.5	3.0	3.3	**3.0**
Emmaus	2	4	3	1	0	0	2	**2.1**

The churches which have been using Alpha or Emmaus longest have tended also to hold the courses the most times. There is therefore a close relationship between the answers to this question and the previous one. Putting them together would suggest that the large majority of churches hold one Alpha or Emmaus course per year.

If the average church has been holding Alpha courses for three years this could mean that they started in 1999 and held them that year and in 2000 and 2001[8]. This suggests that the national advertising in September 1998 helped to stimulate some churches to start holding courses, presumably encouraged by the resources and support available to them, apart from the response generated by the advertising which needed an outlet!

A third, 30%, of the churches have held Alpha only for one year, and a further fifth, 21%, for two years. Another quarter, 26%, have held them for three or four years. That means that almost another quarter, 23%, have held them for more than four years. All this still averages out to one course per year!

How many people came?

How many attended these courses? The question asked for total attendance so numbers will naturally vary by number of courses held. Table 8.7 gives the details in terms of the range of number coming, Table 8.8 the average total number and average per course.

Table 8.7: Number of people attending Alpha and Emmaus courses

Course	Church of Scotland %	Roman Catholic %	Independent %	Smaller denominations %	Baptist %	Other Presbyterian %	Episcopal %	Overall %
1–10	13	25	4	32	23	27	32	20
11–20	27	30	21	33	19	37	14	26
21–30	15	30	21	6	8	18	7	14
31–40	10	5	13	5	11	18	4	10
41–50	6	0	9	5	10	0	18	6
51–75	9	10	13	6	6	0	0	8
76–100	10	0	6	7	15	0	7	9
100+	10	0	13	6	8	0	18	7
1–10	20	0	100	100	–	–	43	39
11–20	40	0	0	0	–	–	43	32
21–30	27	0	0	0	–	–	14	18
30+	13	100	0	0	–	–	0	11

Table 8.8: Average number of people attending in total and per course

	Church of Scotland	Roman Catholic	Independent	Smaller denominations	Baptist	Other Presbyterian	Episcopal	Overall
ALPHA								
In total	47	21	54	33	46	18	54	**40**
Per course	13	10	14	11	11	9	12	**11**
EMMAUS								
In total	22	60	5	5	–	–	12	**18**
Per course	9	10	5	5	–	–	6	**8**

Across the different denominations, on average 40 people have attended Alpha per church across all courses, and 18 Emmaus. This is an average of 11 people per individual Alpha course and 8 for each Emmaus course, that is, larger numbers attend Alpha courses than Emmaus courses.

If the proportions in Table 8.1 also apply to the churches which didn't complete a Census form, then some 1,100 churches in Scotland will have held an Alpha course with a total attendance of 46,800. This is made up of:

- 22,700 or 48% of total in Church of Scotland churches
- 9,300 or 20% of total in Independent churches
- 5,400 or 12% of total in Baptist churches
- 5,000 or 11% of total in Smaller denomination churches
- 2,700 or 6% of total in Episcopal churches
- 1,000 or 2% of total in Roman Catholic churches, and
- 700 or 1% of total in Other Presbyterian churches.

This attendance is equivalent to 0.9% of the total population of Scotland. In addition some 56 churches have held an Emmaus course (a few of these could presumably also have held an Alpha course) with a total attendance of 1,000 people.

Alpha by size of church

Does the likelihood of a church holding an Alpha course vary by its size? The answer is YES, as the graph in Figure 8.9 indicates. Over two-fifths, 43%, of churches with between 151 and 200 attending on a Sunday had held an Alpha course (against an overall average of 27%), and churches with between 51 and 300 were also much more likely to have held a course (average for these churches excluding 151–200 size was 33%). A fifth, 20%, of churches with 50 or fewer had held an Alpha course, and 18% of churches with more than 300 (many of which would be Roman Catholic).

The fact that the largest churches are less likely to have held an Alpha course probably reflects the fact that they already have busy programmes, including effective outreach mechanisms, so that Alpha, while very useful for some, becomes just one of several options and not always chosen. Perhaps smaller churches have fewer options and are therefore more likely to choose to run an Alpha course. The very smallest churches may not have the financial or personnel resources to organise such an event.

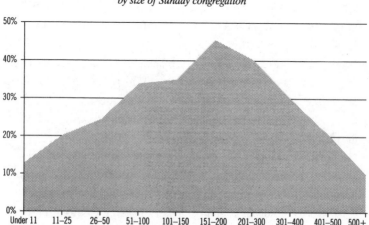

Figure 8.9: Percentage of churches holding an Alpha course by size of Sunday congregation

Alpha and community service

Overall, 57% of churches had members of their congregation involved with community service. But the proportion in churches which had also undertaken an Alpha course was 68%, against 52% of churches which had not had an Alpha course.

This suggests that congregations already involved with the community in whatever way would be more likely to hold an evangelistic teaching course such as Alpha, perhaps not least because they have contacts with people who would be appropriate to invite.

So what does this all say?

In this chapter we have seen:
- Over a quarter, 27%, of churches had held an Alpha course, and just over 1% an Emmaus course.
- Over half the Baptist churches, 58%, had held an Alpha course, but only 8% of Roman Catholic and 11% of Other Presbyterian churches had held one. 4% of the Episcopal churches had held an Emmaus course.
- Over half of Charismatic, 69%, and Reformed Evangelical churches, 52%, had held an Alpha course, but only 9% of Catholic and 14% of Liberal churches had held one. 3% of Liberal churches had held an Emmaus course.
- More than half of suburban churches, 51%, had held an Alpha course, but only a fifth, 20%, of those in New Towns. 3% of Rural Dormitory churches had held an Emmaus course.
- On average Alpha courses had been held four times over 3 years, and Emmaus courses twice in two years.
- On average 11 people attended each Alpha course, 8 each Emmaus course. Courses held by Independent and Church of Scotland churches tended to draw more than average, Other Presbyterian churches slightly fewer. Roman Catholic churches had the highest Emmaus attendance.

- 47,000 people have attended an Alpha course, 1,000 an Emmaus course. This is about 0.9% of the Scottish population who have attended an Alpha course, virtually half, 48%, in a Church of Scotland church.
- The larger the Sunday congregation up to 200, the greater the likelihood of that church having held an Alpha course. Churches larger than 200 are less likely to have done so.
- Churches which had undertaken an Alpha course were more likely to have members of their congregation involved in community service.

NOTES

[1] Details from *Alpha or Emmaus?*, Charles Freebury, thesis for an MA in Evangelism studies at Cliff College, October 2002, Page 6.

[2] *Questions of Life*, Nicky Gumbel, Kingsway, Eastbourne, 1995.

[3] *Alpha Courses: An Appraisal*, Research report for Holy Trinity, Brompton, Peter Brierley, Christian Research, March 2002, Page 32.

[4] Its importance with respect to church growth was explored in Chapter 6.

[5] Op cit. (Footnote 3), Page 7.

[6] The Board of National Mission reported on the impact of Alpha courses at the General Assembly in 1999.

[7] *Church Growth in the 1990s*, Peter Brierley, Research project for Springboard by Christian Research, March 2000.

[8] It might also mean they held them in 1995, 1996 and 1997 and then gave up!

9) Leadership of local congregations

All churches have lay leaders, with various titles. For the first time a question was included which asked Protestant churches the number of Elders, Deacons, Stewards, etc. that served in each church, and for Catholic churches the number of people who participate in Lay Ministries. The type of leadership exercised by these two groups, and certainly the numbers involved in each, vary substantially. It should be noted that these are lay leaders, not ministers, who would need to be added to get total church leadership.

Overall numbers

The average church in Scotland had 18 lay leaders[1]. As there are an estimated 3,100 clergy[2] for Scotland's 4,144 churches, or three ministers for every four churches (a number which excludes curates, associate ministers, etc.), that is, $^3/_4$ clergy per church, we should add another $^3/_4$ to this 18 to get total leadership. For a breakdown of numbers per church, see Table 6.14.

Lay leadership by denomination

The overall figure is misleading, however. The average Church of Scotland church has 27 Elders, the average Catholic church has 29 people in Lay Ministry, and the other churches, which are much closer together in this respect, average between them 6 each. Details by denomination are given in Table 9.1.

If all leaders were to attend church on Sunday, the total of 73,600 lay leaders would be 13% of overall attendance. There have

been a number of books, mostly from the United States, which have
suggested that the ideal number of leaders per church is between
10% and 20% of the total congregation, so this percentage meets
that criterion, but, as Table 9.1 shows, this is largely because of the
high number of Elders in Church of Scotland churches – the Church
of Scotland have twice as many Elders per church as other denominations have lay leaders because their Elders are invariably appointed for life.

Table 9.1: Lay leaders per church, by denomination, 2002

Denomination	Number of churches	Average number per church	Total lay leadership	% of total	% of average congregation
Church of Scotland	1,666	26.9	44,800	*61*	*20*
Roman Catholic	594	29.2	17,300	*24*	*9*
Independent	559	5.5	3,100	*4*	*7*
Smaller denominations	470	4.8	2,300	*3*	*8*
Baptist	204	7.8	1,600	*2*	*6*
Other Presbyterian	342	6.9	2,400	*3*	*11*
Episcopal	309	6.7	2,100	*3*	*11*
Total All Scotland	**4,144**	**17.8**	**73,600**	***100***	*13*

Lay leadership by churchmanship

In what ways do the numbers of lay leaders vary by churchmanship?
Table 9.2 gives the details.

The close link between some denominations and churchmanships comes through in this Table. It is interesting, although perhaps
not surprising because of their ecclesiology, to see that on average
Charismatic Evangelical churches have less than half the number of
lay leaders churches of other persuasions have.

Table 9.2: Lay leaders per church, by churchmanship, 2002

Denomination	Number of churches	Average number per church	Total lay leadership	% of total	% of average congregation
Evan: Mainstream	684	11.4	7,800	11	10
Reformed	667	20.0	13,300	18	16
Catholic	617	22.8	14,100	19	8
Evan: Reformed	594	19.7	11,700	16	22
Broad	573	20.2	11,600	16	19
Liberal	484	18.8	9,100	12	17
Evan: Charismatic	286	6.8	1,900	3	7
Low Church	239	17.2	4,100	5	17
Total All Scotland	**4,144**	**17.8**	**73,600**	**100**	**13**

Leadership by age

The average lay leader is 56 years of age, against an average congregational age of 57. The average age of adults over 25 in the general population of Scotland is 51, so church leaders tend to be older than the overall population. The average age of Scottish ministers is not known, but in the Church of England it is 49[3], which, if true of Scottish clergy, would indicate that lay leadership is on average older than ministerial leadership.

Table 9.3 overleaf gives the percentages in each age-group by denomination and Figure 9.4 graphs these compared with the ages of Sunday congregations.

Two denominations have a third of their lay leaders under 45: the Baptists (33%) and the Catholics (32%). These are followed by the Independents (25%) and the Scottish Episcopal Church (24%). The Presbyterian churches in contrast have only 12% under 45 (Church of Scotland) or 13% (Other Presbyterian), with correspondingly much larger percentages who are 65 or over. Indeed virtually half, 48%, of the Other Presbyterian Elders are 65 and over, and over a third, 36%, of Church of Scotland Elders.

Table 9.3: Age of Scottish lay leaders, by denomination, 2002

Denomination	Under 35 %	35-44 %	45-54 %	55-64 %	65-74 %	75 & over %	Average age LL	AC
Church of Scotland	3	9	21	31	26	10	60	62
Roman Catholic	15	17	25	25	14	4	52	55
Independent	8	17	25	26	16	8	55	56
Smaller denominations	8	12	19	26	28	7	58	57
Baptist	9	24	29	20	15	3	52	51
Other Presbyterian	4	9	17	22	32	16	62	60
Episcopal	10	14	21	33	18	4	54	59
Total All Scotland	9	14	23	27	20	7	56	57

LL: Lay Leaders AC: Adult Congregation

Does the age of lay leadership correlate with church growth or decline? It would seem not. While the denomination with the youngest average age of lay leaders (Deacons) is the Baptists, who are growing, the average age of those in Lay Ministry in the Catholic churches is also 52, and they are declining. The highest average age is amongst the Other Presbyterian churches at 62, and while they are declining, they "only" declined 5% in the period 1994 to 2002, while the Church of Scotland, with Elders on average aged 60, declined 22% in the same period.

Figure 9.4: Average age of lay leaders and adult congregations, 2002

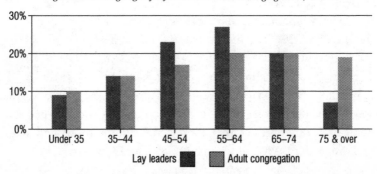

The average age of lay leadership is older than the average age of adult congregations (taken here as 25 and over) for Other Presbyterians, Smaller Denominations and Baptists, as Table 9.3 shows. Across all denominations, however, it is marginally younger than the average age of adult congregations (bottom line of Table 9.3), because the proportion of very old (75 and over) lay leaders is small but a very large proportion (19%, almost a fifth) of Scottish congregations are aged 75 and over (as shown in Table 2.9). If one excluded those who were 75 and over among both leaders and attenders, then it would be seen that there were proportionately too few lay leaders under 45 years of age.

This can be seen also in Table 9.5 which shows the percentage of churches in each age-group who had NO lay leaders of that age.

Table 9.5: Percentage of churches with zero leaders in particular age-groups, 2002

Denomination	Under 35 %	35–44 %	45–54 %	55–64 %	65–74 %	75/75+ %
Church of Scotland	68	39	25	20	20	42
Roman Catholic	55	52	41	41	54	78
Independent	81	66	50	52	60	82
Smaller denominations	83	71	61	51	54	82
Baptist	61	41	27	37	44	83
Other Presbyterian	84	73	58	52	36	53
Episcopal	82	73	62	57	64	86
Total All Scotland	74	61	48	46	48	73

That three-quarters of Scottish churches have no lay leaders under 35 years of age suggests problems for the future! Is this because too few under-35s attend, or because they are deemed to have insufficient experience, or not to have the relevant gifts? Or is it because they are too busy in their normal employment or family life to have the time for leadership? If appointed, might they be too revolutionary? It would seem important to know.

Lay leadership and growth

Churches were asked to indicate whether they thought their church would have grown or declined by 2010. Was the number of leaders per church significant in this context? Against an all-Scotland average of 18 leaders per church, there were on average:

- 13 in churches which expected significant growth
- 18 in churches which expected to grow a little
- 21 in churches which expected to remain stable
- 20 in churches which expected to decline, and
- 6 in churches which expected to close.

This suggests that churches which are on the point of closing find it difficult to recruit new leadership, and that churches which consider themselves likely to grow have a smaller leadership base. Churches with the largest average numbers of leaders were those expecting to remain stable or decline.

Lay leadership and finance

Another question asked churches if in the past year their finance had grown, remained stable or declined. Were the number of lay leaders related to these answers? There were on average:

- 19 lay leaders in churches where the finance had increased
- 16 lay leaders in churches where the finance was stable, and
- 16 lay leaders in churches where the finance had declined.

There is no strong correlation here, though the results suggest that the more lay leaders a church has the better its finances!

So what does this all say?

This chapter is about the number of lay leaders in churches, not what they do nor how effective they are. The role they play vis-a-vis ordained leadership is not explored either. This chapter has shown:

- On average, Scottish churches have 18 lay leaders per church. This is an amalgam of 29 in Catholic Lay Ministries, 27 Elders in Church of Scotland parishes, and 6 each in other denominations.
- On average, Elders in Church of Scotland churches comprise one-fifth of the entire congregation, a percentage at least double that in other churches.
- Charismatic Evangelical churches seem to require less than half the average number of lay leaders that other churches need.
- The average age of leaders and adult members of congregations is much the same, but Presbyterian churches have a much higher percentage of Elders over 65 than lay leaders in other churches, presumably because most Elders are appointed for life.
- That three-quarters of Scottish churches have no lay leaders under 35 years of age suggests problems for the future! It would be useful to ascertain the reasons for this.
- Churches expecting to close have far fewer leaders than others. Churches expecting to grow significantly have only two-thirds the number of leaders in slowly growing, stable or declining churches. Do fewer leaders help facilitate growth?
- More leaders are marginally associated with growing finance.

The comparisons between denominations in this chapter are important. Would the Church of Scotland fare better if its Elders were not appointed for life, but had a tenure of, say, seven years, and had to retire for at least 12 months before they could be voted in again? If fewer leaders are needed for churches expecting to grow, should churches seek to reduce their leadership team to people who can really lead rather than just fulfil a leadership role?[4]

But probably the greatest challenge that emerges is the small percentage of younger lay leaders. Are there possible candidates in the churches, or have they already left? Are they so busy in secular work that they don't have time to take up church leadership? Have they simply never been asked to lead? It is hard to believe that in some churches there are so few with the gift of leadership.

NOTES

[1] There were a small number of churches who said they had a very large number of lay leaders. Whether this was because the number entered was incorrect or the question was misunderstood is not known, but to prevent these large numbers affecting the average, churches indicating they had more than 100 lay leaders were excluded from the general calculations in this chapter.

[2] *Religious Trends,* No 1, 1998/1999, Christian Research, London and Paternoster Publishing, Carlisle, 1997, Table 2.6.

[3] *Religious Trends,* No 2, 2000/2001, Christian Research and HarperCollins, London, 1999, Page 5.4.

[4] This question makes a number of assumptions about the role of existing leaders which may not be justified!

10) What the people said

Contributed by Heather Wraight

The Census data which has been analysed in the previous chapters reveals an enormous amount about churches in Scotland. However, the Census Steering Committee felt it was important to try to find out some of the reasons behind the trends revealed by the quantitative study.

Four Focus Groups were planned in order to explore in depth some of the factors shown up by the preliminary analyses of the Census results. These were held in Hamilton (city suburb/dormitory town, west), Glasgow (city centre, west), Glenrothes (new town, east), Arbroath (rural town, east).

The Focus Groups were attended by people of different ages, both genders and a wide range of denominations (but with more from the Church of Scotland and Roman Catholic Church as these are the largest denominations). Except for the Glasgow group which was organised at short notice, there was a spread of experiences of church. In all, 38 people attended the four groups.

Background Information

In order to make sure that those invited met the criteria a selection questionnaire was distributed in advance. This also provided the opportunity to gather additional information. One question asked whether in their opinion more or fewer people attended their church than two years ago, and if so why. The Minister/Priest, or lack of one, appeared as a reason both for more and for fewer people attending

– he or she clearly affects the whole congregation either positively or negatively.

Virtually all the churches which were thought to be growing had a range of activities and some form of outreach into, or contact with, the local community, whereas those which were declining did not have such involvement. In the growing congregations people were enthusiastic and welcoming, whereas other congregations were losing elderly people and not replacing them. The changing nature of Sunday was also a negative influence. These factors have been observed elsewhere, in a study of churches in England which are growing[1].

Another question with interesting results asked about their childhood attendance, whether at church or Sunday School, and if they had stopped attending, at what age that had been. It was quite surprising to find that 15 of the 38 had dropped out at some point, 11 of whom had returned later. This suggests that there are many others who used to go to church and don't now, but could be drawn back. This pattern of dropping out is repeating itself with their own children: all the primary aged ones attend but few older ones.

Attendance

Table 10.1: Attendance on Sunday (or Saturday Mass for Catholics)

Frequency	Total
Usually every week	32
Two or three times a month	2
Once a month	1
Less than once a month	1
Special occasions only	0
Almost never	2

The 1998 English Church Attendance Survey found that significant numbers of people were attending church less often than they used to. At the time of undertaking the Focus Groups the data on frequency in Scotland had not yet been analysed so it was not known whether Scotland had followed the same pattern as England. However, the opportunity was taken to explore the attendance pattern of these people and others in their congregation. Sunday attendance, weekly if possible, was still the norm for most.

1) Attendance at a midweek worship service

All the Catholic churches represented had at least one midweek Mass, some of them daily. All the Catholics in the groups attended at least on special occasions, while two went daily, one when she was working on Sunday, and another once or twice a week. Only two of the Protestant churches offered a midweek worship service on a regular basis. Some others had midweek worship on special occasions such as Ascension Day or for ecumenical events, but most almost never provide an opportunity to worship at any time other than Sunday.

Most of the Catholics thought that perhaps three or four people attended their church midweek who did not attend on Sunday. One of the Protestant churches estimated that perhaps 10% of its midweek attenders did not come on Sunday, while the other did not know.

The very few opportunities for Protestants to worship midweek was felt by most to be a lack. The Catholics observed that their midweek services, while mainly attended by older people also attracted younger people whose jobs did not allow them to worship on Sunday. Most of the Protestants in these Focus Groups would welcome the availability of midweek worship, even if they personally did not wish to attend then.

2) Attendance at other midweek activities

The picture here was exactly the opposite to midweek worship: some Catholic churches had the Exposition of the Sacrament, but there was little else offered by any. The Protestant churches on the other hand had a wide range of activities between them including: prayer meeting, Bible study, home groups of various kinds, Alpha Courses or similar, youth and/or children's activities, choir, drama group and social events, as well as elders or deacons meetings. It was noticeable that the older people were much more likely to go to at least one of these and often more, while those with young families were unlikely to go to anything mostly because they were too busy, too tired after work, or actually at work.

When asked what they would choose to attend at their church if they could only go to *one* thing, almost everyone opted for Sunday morning worship, with one or two preferring Sunday evening. Sunday is clearly still perceived as *the* day for church.

3) Personal Change in Attendance

The attendance of the majority had not changed but there were some in each group, in addition to those who had started or stopped recently, whose attendance had altered in the last two or three years. The reasons given for attending more often than two years ago were all to do with two factors: either they liked what was going on at their church and wished to be part of it, or a change in personal circumstances such as retirement giving more time to attend or to take grandchildren to church whose parents had dropped out. Those who had joined recently all had some kind of faith experience or conversion.

Some of those who were attending less often were mothers of young children and/or mothers who had started working. It became clear from various comments both at this point in the groups and at other times that young mothers are under particular pressures not shared in quite the same way by other groups in society. These affect church attendance in several ways:

• A growing number of young women remain in full-time employ-ment after marriage and increasingly also after children are born. The opinion expressed was that women can cope with full-time work, marriage and church, but when children are born they can-not add the demands of a baby as well. Something has to go, and church attendance is the most likely activity to be dropped or at least to decline in frequency.

- Many of the jobs created by Sunday trading are filled by women, a large proportion of them being in retail. Although Sunday trading in Scotland has been permitted for much longer than in England, the respondents' opinion was that it had increased considerably in the last few years, which presumably requires either more staff or staff to work longer hours.
- A change in the church attendance patterns for women is more likely to affect the attendance of their children than a change in the attendance patterns of men. One woman observed that in her church if a man was working on Sunday his wife was likely to attend and bring the children, but if the wife was working her husband was unlikely to attend and bring the children. Others in that group agreed with her.
- Women aged over 45 rarely have young children. Therefore even if they are in full-time employment they are likely to be able to continue to cope with including church attendance in their week.

The decline in attendance of children has previously been thought to be due to a decline in attendance by parents. While this is presumably true in many cases, the corollary is also part of the picture: <u>some parents' attendance declines *because* they have children.</u> When there are too many demands, church attendance is deemed less essential than work, children or marriage, so it is often the activity which goes by default.

4) Changes in Attendance

All groups were asked to list on a flip chart the main reasons first for starting to attend a church in that part of Scotland and secondly for leaving. People were then given votes so that the items could be prioritised. The factors can be grouped into several categories, many of which have been observed in previous studies. The number in brackets is the number of votes received by each item across all four groups.

Reasons for people starting to attend church were thought to be: warmth of welcome or sense of family (32), Spiritual journey

(30), occasional offices (27), mission and outreach (24), children's or youth activities (18), relationship factors (14), the impact of the minister (6), quality of the worship (6), moving house (5), switching church (5), personal life crisis or changing life stage (2). Other factors which were listed but not given any votes were: welcoming to particular groups, students, people's mobility, location of the church, facilities for special needs, Alpha, elderly facing big issues.

Reasons for people stopping attending were perceived as: the demands of employment and the pressures of life (26), church being irrelevant or boring (24), disagree with the attitudes or teaching of the church (22), changing attitudes in society (21), the other activities available on Sunday especially for children(15), young people dropping out because of peer pressure or the freedom to choose not to go (13), not meeting their needs (13), personal life crisis or changing life stage (12), the impact of the minister (9), elderly die (8), loss of faith (8), personality clashes (7), disagree with changes in worship/liturgy (6), lack of welcome (4), scandal in the church (3), moving away (2). Other factors which were listed but not given any votes were: people feel slighted, out of fashion.

Clearly the groups felt more strongly about the reasons why people stopped attending, as there are 30 votes too many in this category! In other words they used up their votes too quickly but voted anyway for other factors they agreed with.

West versus East

The lower church attendance in the south and east of Scotland (see Chapter 3) had been thought to be due to cultural factors – perhaps the Celtic background more common in the north and west had encouraged continued church attendance. However, an illuminating discussion at Arbroath suggested it is due rather to negative social relationship factors which are more prevalent in the south and east.

Personality clashes and interpersonal relationships appeared on the stopping list for both groups in the east and neither in the west. The facilitator had observed that personality clashes had received some votes in Glenrothes but had not been mentioned in either Hamilton or Glasgow. So when they were proposed in Arbroath the group was asked whether they thought personality clashes were more likely in the east than the west of Scotland. The response was immediately affirmative! It was felt that there was a certain 'pricklyness' about people on the east coast which those who came from or had lived in the west had not found there.

More knowledge of the social and psychological differences between east and west Scotland is needed to know whether this is indeed a significant factor, but it would be worth exploring.

Changes since 1994

The previous Scottish Church Census took place in 1994. All groups were therefore asked which of the factors on their lists of starting or stopping attending would have been different then and whether those changes were particularly relevant to certain age groups or gender. These responses are sufficiently thought provoking to be worth listing in full.

1) Positive Changes affecting Reasons for Starting to Attend
- Pastoral care, especially at times of bereavement was perceived to have improved – are ministers better trained for it? – resulting in more older people returning to church after attending a funeral.
- More churches seem to have youth work, which should result in more young people attending, or at least fewer leaving.
- Alpha Courses are new, or at least much more widespread, since 1994 and there is also a growth in other courses being run by churches. These bring adults of all ages into contact with the church.

- Music – people are more discerning about music and will therefore come for good music, although they will also be put off by poor music. Young people sometimes stay in church if they are part of a music group or band – but this may have happened longer ago than 1994.
- Legislation requiring churches (along with other public buildings) to provide for people with special needs should make them more attractive.
- One of the churches represented was now open all day, providing many contacts as people came in to talk.
- Most groups discussed warmth of welcome, with some feeling it was improving but others disagreeing. There was a general feeling among 'incomers' to an area that they were not always welcome, and this was especially true for one attender who was English and the English husband of another who felt less welcome since Scottish Devolution!

2) Negative Changes affecting Reasons for Starting to Attend
- Fewer couples now get married, so fewer make contact with a church for that purpose. This particularly affects young adults.
- More activities on Sunday means there is much more choice of things to do, especially for children and young people. Many of the alternatives are more attractive.
- Religious Education in schools is more multifaith, so there are fewer opportunities to make contact with young people through ministers taking RE lessons.
- More women working, especially young mothers (see above).

3) Positive Changes affecting Reasons for Stopping Attending
- There are more youth workers in churches so fewer young people leave because there is nothing for them.

- Likewise, more youth workers result in a better understanding of young people by older people [although this was <u>not</u> the impression gained from a different research project which held Focus Groups with church youth workers in Scotland[2]].
- There has been an increase in different kinds of services – younger people saw this as positive, but older as negative!

4) Negative Changes affecting Reasons for Stopping Attending
- The demands of jobs have increased with more of those in work feeling under pressure and often exhausted by the time they get home from work. This is especially true for working mothers and young fathers.
- Many jobs no longer offer a choice about whether or not an employee works on Sunday.
- There are many more alternative activities on Sunday, especially Sunday sport for children.
- Changes in education mean children and young people have shorter attention spans so it is more difficult to keep their interest and attention in church.
- Scandals, especially involving Catholic priests, are more open and known about, affecting the public's perceptions of the denomination, and parents' willingness to allow their children to attend.
- Society has become more secular and more materialistic resulting in fewer people seeing the church as relevant to their lives, except perhaps in times of national or personal crisis.

Children & Young People

This section of the Focus Groups was originally intended only for parents of children of two age groups, under 11 and 11 to 18. However, in all the groups most of the older people had grandchildren of these ages and so joined in the discussion also.

1) Under 11s

Nearly all the children in this age group attended church with their parents, but two older ones were now allowed to choose whether they attended, and while both still did they no longer came every Sunday. Not all the grandchildren attended, and this was invariably because their parents did not attend. However, one family of grandchildren attended with their grandparents, a factor which was noticed in a survey in England[3].

All of the children were thought to enjoy attending most of the time. The Catholic children enjoyed Children's Liturgy but did not enjoy church as much on the Sundays when they were expected to attend the adult service – indeed a couple of parents only took their children on Sundays when they would be able to attend Children's Liturgy. This suggests that Catholic churches should be encouraged to hold Children's Liturgy on more Sundays and in more churches.

When asked whether parents or grandparents thought these children would still be attending by the time they were, say, 15, the answer was an almost unanimous yes – *if* there were suitable youth activities which they enjoyed, but otherwise no.

2) 11 to 18 year olds

Perhaps not surprisingly fewer of these attended but most of those who did enjoyed it – if their friends went as well. It seemed they were more likely to still be attending in a smaller town where their friends lived nearby so they could attend together. In the larger conurbation of Hamilton and Glasgow friends from school were more likely to live further away so if a friend went to church it would almost certainly be a different one. Neither parents nor grandparents had as much influence on their attendance at this age.

Would they still be attending by the time they were, say, 25? "It depends" was the common answer – on whether they get involved and whether their friends continue to go. If the answer to both of these was yes then the parents and grandparents expected they would continue to attend, but not otherwise.

Both parents and grandparents believe that their children's or grandchildren's continued attendance depends on the provision of suitable youth activities, whether their friends attend, and involving older children and young people in the life of the church. The first and third of these factors are within the control of churches.

3) Reasons for children and young people leaving

While the previous items were being discussed, the facilitator noted factors which were mentioned as reasons for children or young people to leave church. Respondents were then asked if they wished to add any others, and the resulting list was prioritised and scored (the number in brackets being the total score all groups).

Across the four Focus Groups two kinds of reasons emerged as to why children and young people drop out:

a) their own experiences as they grow up: becoming independent and making their own decisions (38), the changing nature of Sunday ($29^1/_2$), the move to and pressures of Secondary School (20), peer pressure ($18^1/_2$), family attitudes (17).

b) their attitudes towards church: including the perceived irrelevance of church (39), no youth activities or other provision for them (23) and the lack of friends their own age at church (14).

Attractive Aspects of Church Life

Respondents were then given a pack of 20 cards each with a word or phrase describing a possible aspect of church life. Half of these were intended as positive descriptions and half as negative. They were asked to select three words or phrases which best described the kind of church which they thought would attract non-churchgoers, and which three were most likely to put off non-churchgoers. The Table on the next page splits very neatly into four groups of five:

a) the top group have a high impact in attracting non-churchgoers – it could be said that they are what constitute good practice for churches.

b) the next five have a low impact in attracting non-churchgoers.
c) the third group have a low impact in putting off non-churchgoers.
d) the bottom five factors have a high impact in putting off
   non-churchgoers and are in effect bad practice for churches.

Table 10.2: Factors most or least likely to attract newcomers to church

Factor	Most likely	Least likely
Good worship	25	0
Activities for children	21	0
Relevant preaching	18	0
Lots going on	17	0
Caring to people in the community	14	0
Caring to attenders	7	0
Full of new ideas	4	1
Prayerful	3	0
Mission-minded	1	0
Professional	1	0
Uncomfortable physically	0	4
Difficult to make friends	0	5
Impersonal	0	8
Institutional	0	8
Mostly elderly attenders	0	8
Always asking for money	0	13
Narrow-minded	0	13
Out of touch	0	16
Old-fashioned	0	17
Boring	0	21

Leaving Church

In the groups there were a few people who had either completely stopped attending church or were attending much less than they used to. They were asked why they had left, and then everyone was asked whether they had ever thought of leaving church themselves, and if so what the reason(s) had been. The reasons for leaving, or considering doing so were: a time of personal crisis, a lack of personal support, too many demands made in a small or ageing con-gregation where there were not enough people to do everything, personality clashes, theological conflicts and a new minister who changed things.

Church growth

Research amongst growing and larger Protestant churches in England has revealed a number of factors which are common to each, or distinctive in either a growing or a larger church. A dozen of these factors were selected and each attender was asked to score their own church on a scale of 1 to 10 for each factor, where 1 is very poor and 10 is excellent. In this way an overall score for each factor was obtained. Each form also asked the person to state their denom-ination and so average scores for the denomination represented could be obtained, though numbers are very small for three.

Table 10.3: Scores for growth factors

Factor	Overall	Catholic	Church of Scotland	Baptist	Independent	United Reformed	Scottish Episcopal
Number of respondents	**38**	11	14	8	2	2	1
Relevance of the preaching	**8.1**	7.2	8.3	8.9	9.0	8.0	8.0
Friendliness of the people	**8.1**	8.3	7.8	8.3	9.0	9.0	6.0
Strong leader/minister	**8.0**	7.1	8.4	7.9	10.0	8.0	8.0
Chance to belong to a 'family'	**7.9**	7.1	8.1	9.1	9.5	7.0	7.0
Quality of the worship	**7.8**	7.1	8.1	8.3	7.5	9.0	9.0
Warmth of the welcome	**7.5**	5.9	7.8	8.3	9.0	8.0	7.0
Presence of people of all ages	**7.3**	6.2	6.9	8.9	10.0	8.0	5.0
Clear vision of church's direction	**6.8**	5.8	7.0	7.4	8.5	6.0	6.0
Range of children's activities	**6.3**	3.8	7.7	8.3	8.5	2.5	1.0
Opportunity to be anonymous	**6.0**	7.0	6.4	6.0	3.0	1.5	9.0
Programmes serving community	**5.8**	3.9	6.7	7.0	6.5	3.0	3.0
Evangelism involving social action	**5.7**	3.7	5.6	7.3	9.0	3.0	4.0
Overall	**7.1**	**6.1**	**7.9**	**8.0**	(8.3)	(6.0)	(6.2)

This shows interesting variations. However, an additional – and much more significant – analysis was made possible by comparing answers on these questionnaires with the selection questionnaires which had asked whether the person attended a church which they considered to be growing, stable or declining. The overall column is repeated for ease of comparison.

Table 10.4: Scores for growth factors by growth or decline of church

Factor	Overall	Growing	Stable	Declining
Number of responses	38	11	14	11
Relevance of the preaching	8.1	9.5	8.3	6.5
Friendliness of the people	8.1	8.7	8.5	7.2
Strong leader/minister	8.0	9.2	8.3	6.4
Chance to belong to a 'family'	7.9	9.3	7.4	7.8
Quality of the worship	7.8	9.3	8.0	6.5
Warmth of the welcome	7.5	8.7	7.2	6.6
Presence of people of all ages	7.3	8.7	6.6	6.7
Clear vision of church's direction	6.8	8.6	6.4	5.5
Range of children's activities	6.3	8.3	6.3	4.3
Opportunity to be anonymous	6.0	6.6	5.1	5.8
Programmes serving local community	5.8	7.2	6.1	3.1
Evangelism involving social action	5.7	7.7	5.3	3.7
Overall	7.1	8.5	7.0	5.9

This is clear evidence, albeit from a small sample, that the factors identified in the studies of growing or larger churches are indeed significant. The difference in score between the churches which are growing and those which are declining is very great, especially on factors near the bottom of the list where the growing churches continued to score above the overall average while the declining churches were much lower. The factor which met with least approval among these respondents in growing churches was 'Opportunity to be anonymous', a factor found in the other studies to be relevant to larger churches but not to smaller, growing ones. This also confirms that finding.

Conclusion

To conclude the Focus Group and help attenders sum up their thoughts during the evening they were asked three final questions. What they liked most about belonging to a church brought a very wide range of answers, with the most common being the sense of family (9). Other things mentioned by more than one person were a feeling of belonging (4), fellowship (4), feeling close to God/the Holy Spirit (4), worship (2) and being taught God's word (2).

What they liked least about belonging to a church also had clear 'winners' and a range of other answers with these given by more than one person: cliques (17), the politics and pettiness (9), divisions between denominations (4), and lack of commitment by many (2).

People and relationships are therefore both most liked and least liked, depending on whether they draw people together or drive them apart. Working at relationships is thus very important for churches.

The final question asked those present what one thing churches in Scotland should do to attract more people to church. Replies fell into five groups:

- *Leaders and services.* They wanted ministers and priests to communicate better and address real issues from a biblical perspective. They would also encourage them to recognise and use the gifts of the congregation and get to know their needs and pressures.
- *Structures and buildings.* There was considerable frustration at the length of time it takes for denominations to make and implement decisions. Many church buildings were considered old fashioned, ill equipped and thus a barrier to people coming for the first time. They wanted to encourage churches to get out of the past.
- *Be more ecumenical.* They would like churches to both work and pray together.
- *Current congregations.* Churches need to be better at welcoming new people and encourage current attenders to get stuck in.

• *Outreach.* Some strong opinions were expressed about the way churches seem to expect non-churchgoers to become "like us" before they come. They believe churches should meet people where they are, at a level they can relate to, get more involved in the community and find ways to welcome groups which are usually excluded from church. They also want appropriate outreach to young people, such as Christian raves.

These lay people had plenty of ideas of how churches in Scotland could change. Some expressed the hope that they would be listened to more often.

Findings directly related to trends revealed in the results

• *A decline in numbers of people aged 30 to 44,* ie the age when people are most likely to be parents. Some parents' attendance declines *because* they have children. When there are too many demands, church attendance is deemed less essential than either work, children or marriage, so it is often the activity which goes by default. This is probably the key reason for the decline in attendance of people aged 30 to 44, as well as the reason why more women have left church than men.

• *A greater loss of women of working age than of men.* More of the jobs created by Sunday trading are filled by women than by men. Although Scotland has had Sunday trading for much longer than England, the groups observed that the amount of Sunday trading had increased considerably in recent years. Jobs in retail are more likely to employ women, and as more women enter the employment market, more of them work on Sunday.

- *An increase in numbers of attenders aged 65 and over.* It is suspected, but not confirmed, that this is also related to work pressures. Those who had returned aged 65 or over did so after retiring because they now have time to attend church. Those who have returned may not consider themselves to have dropped out entirely eg the Church of Scotland members might still have attended Communion but not gone on a weekly basis.
- *A difference in attendance between the west and north of Scotland and the south and east.* This would appear to be because of cultural differences. It seems likely that people in the east of Scotland are less welcoming to 'incomers' than those in the West, and more likely to take offence at changes in church practice or be driven to leave church because of a personality clash. This deserves further study.

Other significant Focus Group findings

- The Minister/Priest, or lack of one, affects the whole congregation either positively or negatively.
- 15 of the 38 people had dropped out at some point after attending as a child, 11 of whom had come back. This suggests that there more people who could be drawn back to church.
- People and relationships are the most liked thing about being part of a church – if they draw people together. They are the least liked thing about being part of a church if they drive them apart.
- There is a lack of opportunities for Protestants to worship mid-week. Most of the Protestants in these Focus Groups would welcome the availability of midweek worship.
- Catholic churches should be encouraged to hold Children's Liturgy on more Sundays and in more churches.

- There are two types of reasons why children and young people drop out:
  a) their own experiences as they grow up
  b) the perceived irrelevance of church especially where no provision is made for them.
- Good practice for churches wishing to attract non-churchgoers is to provide good worship, activities for children, relevant preaching, lots going on, care to people in the community.
- Bad practice for churches wishing to attract non-churchgoers includes always asking for money and being narrow-minded, out of touch, old fashioned and boring.
- There is clear evidence, albeit from a small sample, that the factors identified in the two studies of growing and of larger churches are indeed significant.
- The participants in these groups were all lay people. They appreciated being consulted, showed they had many ideas about the reasons behind the decline in attendance and what could be done about it, and expressed the hope that their respective churches would listen to people like them more often.

NOTES

[1] Private research for Salvation Army Central North Division, Christian Research, 2002.
[2] Focus Groups as part of research for Church of Scotland on why 11 to 14 year olds leave church, Christian Research, 2000
[3] *Reaching & Keeping Tweenagers,* Peter Brierley, Christian Research, London, 2002.

Executive Summary
and Recommendations

It is easy to be humorous about aspects of church life in Scotland, such as when someone pointed out that an anagram of Presbyterians is Britney Spears and an anagram of Episcopal is Pepsi-Cola – to which someone replied that an anagram of the Houses of Parliament was the Loonies Far Up Thames![1]

The reality however is much more serious, and needs to be taken seriously also. The 2002 Scottish Church Census has built on previous studies, but extended the questions asked. It has also been able to build on past studies to evaluate key trends, and to do this in a statistical manner to demonstrate significant consequences. A viable response, 52%, was achieved. [Chapter 1]

1) *Numbers.* There are still a considerable number of people attending church, far more than almost any other voluntary activity. For instance league football in Scotland only attracts 4.5% of the Scottish population. However, the number of people attending church in Scotland dropped 18% between 1994 and 2002 to reach a 2002 total of 570,000 people, or 11.2% of the population. The sheer scale of the decline has to be of major concern as the implications are so great. The Baptists were the only major denomination to grow, and they did so by only 1%. Three-fifths, 58%, of Scottish churchgoers attend church at least once every week, equivalent to 6.5% of the entire population. [Chapter 2]

2) *Growth.* The Focus Groups showed that clear vision, good leadership and relevant preaching are hallmarks of growing churches. The importance of vision and leadership (as measured by smaller numbers of lay leaders) emerged as the key factors of all those examined for Scotland in the 21st century. Three-fifths, 57%, of congregations are expecting to grow by 2010. [Chapters 2, 6 and 10]

3) *Size.* Congregations are getting smaller, rather than churches closing in line with declining numbers. The average Protestant Sunday congregation in 2002 was 104, Catholics 340; they had been 124 and 418 in 1994. However, some churches are large. A fifth (including the Catholics), 22%, have more than 200. 50% of Scottish churchgoers attend just 15% of churches. [Chapter 2]

4) *Those leaving.* Huge numbers of young people (under 30) have dropped out of church in the last 20 years in Scotland, as in England and other Western countries. It is those who are now in their 60s who have dropped out least; the attendance of older people in their 70s has declined, but for natural reasons. The proportions of those aged 15 to 64 who left between 1994 and 2002 have all increased starkly against the decreases seen between 1984 and 1994. The key reason for this has been the extra numbers of women leaving the church. [Chapters 2, 4 and 10]

5) *Areas of high attendance.* The areas which are seeing church attendance at much higher levels are where the Roman Catholic Church is especially strong, or, where the Free Church of Scotland is strong as in the case of the Western Isles (Eilean Siar), Skye and Lochalsh, where two out of five in the population, 39%, attend church on Sunday. The western and north western parts of Scotland have maintained a higher churchgoing rate than the eastern and southern parts over the years 1984 to 2002. This would appear to be at least partly due to cultural factors. [Chapters 3 and 10]

6) *Older people.* The number of people attending church aged 65 or over has marginally increased between 1994 and 2002 (as it did in England). Compared with the population, however, the church has twice as many people 65 and over, and only half the percentage of those in their 20s. The different generations need to be reached in ways relevant to the culture of their age-group. [Chapter 4]

7) *Gender.* There were slightly more men in church in 1994 than 1984, and slightly more women in church in 2002 than in 1994. Because women are leaving the church at a faster rate than men, the proportion of men in the church has increased from 37% in 1984 to 40% in 2002. This increase is seen across all age groups between 15 and 64. Women are leaving because of the pressure of working full-time combined with marriage and having children. [Chapters 4 and 10]

8) *Congregational age.* The Church of Scotland (51) and the Episcopal Church (50) have the highest percentage of those 65 and over, and consequently the highest average age (shown in brackets). The Baptists on the other hand have the highest percentage of all denominations of people aged 30 to 44, and the lowest average age (40). [Chapter 4]

9) *Future.* If the present trends continue, the future of Scottish church life is bleak, as the church becomes increasingly elderly (the average age goes up to 56 in 2020) and a smaller and smaller percentage of the population attend (under 7% by 2020). Urgent, strategic action is needed in all churches if these forecasts are not to become reality. [Chapter 4]

10) *Churchmanship.* Only the Mainstream Evangelical church-manship wing of the churches in Scotland grew between 1994 and 2002, as in England also. This came mostly through the Church of Scotland, Independent and Other Presbyterian churches. Charismatics have by far the youngest age profile, and Broad, Liberal, Low Church and Reformed by far the oldest. [Chapter 5]

11) *Environment.* While a third of Scottish churchgoers attend churches in towns, it is the suburban churches, to which a sixth go, which have decreased least in the 8 years to 2002. Apart from the Church of Scotland and Roman Catholic Church, all the other denominations saw growth in their City Centre congregations during the second half of the 1990s. [Chapter 5]

12) *Midweek services.* 56% of Scottish churches (42% in England) have a midweek service. Average attendance was 27 (21 in England), with the Catholics having the largest numbers, adding a further 0.6% of the population to the worshipping community in Scotland. These were more likely to be 65 and over and less likely to be aged 20 to 44, compared with Sunday attenders. The majority, 56%, of churches had just one such service, frequently on a Wednesday at 7.00 pm. Protestants would like more opportunities for midweek worship. [Chapters 7 and 10]

13) *Provision for youth.* Almost half, 47%, of the churches held youth activities midweek, with a majority, 63%, of Baptist churches, and 59% of Church of Scotland churches doing so. 102,000 young people are involved in total, 6.6% of the relevant population, 1.7% of the total population; seven-eighths of these, 86%, do not attend church on Sunday. Two-thirds are in Church of Scotland youth activities, proportionately more under 15 attending these clubs than children attending church on Sunday. The most popular club day was Fridays, at 6.00 pm. Parents believe their children are more likely to continue to attend church if there is good provision of youth activities. [Chapters 7 and 10]

14) *Fringe events.* A third, 33%, of churches (45% in England) had "fringe" events, church-led midweek activities attended by those who did not normally attend Sunday worship. Independent churches were particularly strong here, with 80% holding such. Average attendance was 73 people, 41 adults and 32 children, totalling 1.6% of the population. Midweek activities are more likely to attract women than men. [Chapter 7]

15) *Community work.* More than half the churches, 57%, have members of their congregation involved with community service, care and welfare groups. This involves about one-sixth of their congregation, 16%, on average. Episcopal and Church of Scotland congregations are most likely to be involved in such community groups, as are the Liberals and Charismatic Evangelicals. [Chapter 7]

16) *Population and church.* While 11.2% of the population attend church on Sunday, up to a further 0.6% attend midweek. In addition 1.7% attend midweek church youth activities and another 1.6% other such activities. So a total of 15.1% of the Scottish population interacts with the churches each week, three-quarters, 74%, on a Sunday. Thus, for every three people in church on Sunday, another attends a midweek activity. [Chapter 7]

17) *Alpha and Emmaus courses.* Over a quarter, 27%, of churches had held an Alpha course, and just over 1% an Emmaus course. Over half, 58%, of the Baptist churches had held an Alpha course, and 4% of the Episcopal churches had held an Emmaus course. More than half of suburban churches, 51%, had held an Alpha course. On average Alpha courses had been held 4 times over 3 years, and Emmaus courses twice in two years, with an average attendance of 11 people at Alpha and 8 at Emmaus. This amounts to 47,000 people having attended an Alpha course, about 0.9% of the Scottish population, and 1,000 an Emmaus course. Churches which had undertaken an Alpha course were more likely to have members of their congregation involved in community service. [Chapter 8]

18) *Lay leadership.* On average, Scottish churches have 18 lay leaders per church. This is an amalgam of 29 in Catholic Lay Ministries, 27 Elders in Church of Scotland parishes (one-fifth of their congregation), and 6 each in other denominations. Charismatic Evangelical churches have less than half the average number of lay leaders of other churches. Three-quarters of Scottish churches have no lay leaders under 35 years of age. Churches expecting to close have far fewer leaders than others. Churches expecting to grow significantly have only two-thirds the average number of leaders, supporting the hypothesis that fewer leaders facilitate growth. [Chapter 9]

19) *Finance.* Just over three-fifths, 62%, of churches reported that their financial giving had increased over the past year. This was particularly associated with growing churches. In only 8% had giving decreased. [Chapter 4]

20) *Expectations of change.* A fifth, 20%, of churches expected to grow significantly by 2010, and nearly twice as many, 37%, to have grown a little. A further fifth, 22%, reckoned they would remain stable, but another fifth, 19%, that they would decline. 2% of Scottish churches said they would have closed in the next 8 years. [Chapter 4]

All this amounts to a serious, and deteriorating, situation. Churches are shrinking, younger people and women are leaving. If present trends continue, less than 7% of the population will be attending church by 2020. Midweek and youth services are popular with some, as are other midweek activities, but three-quarters of church people in Scotland associate church with Sunday attendance. The key factors for growth relate to vision and leadership; the fewer lay leaders the better, although there is a drastic shortage of young leaders.

The key recommendations emerging from this Census therefore relate to the importance of streamlining leadership (particularly enabling Elders in the Church of Scotland to hand over to a smaller and younger group), and training the remainder in strategic thinking and vision building. That must also include relating the message to contemporary culture, making it relevant to each age-group, and continuing to experiment with midweek events, and courses like Alpha and Emmaus.

NOTE

[1] Correspondence in the *Daily Telegraph* 15th October 2002.

Appendix 1

SCOTTISH CHURCH CENSUS

BASIC INFORMATION

1. Name of Church/Fellowship if different from above _____
   Denomination _____

2. Postal Address of Church if different from above _____
   _____

3. Name of Minister/Priest/Leader _____
   Phone No _____ Email _____ (in case of queries)

4. Is the person named in question 3 responsible for other congregations as well?
   YES ☐ / NO ☐   If YES, how many? _____
   A form should have been received for each church for which this person is responsible. If not, please write below the details of other churches or attach a list so that we can check our records.
   Name _____
   Town/Village _____

ATTENDANCE

5. Please indicate the total attendance at this church on Saturday/Sunday 11/12 May 2002. If there was no service on 11/12 May 2002, please give instead figures for the most recent Sunday on which the congregation met for worship.

   Total number of adults (aged 15 and above) attending all Sunday services. ☐

   Estimated number of adults attending more than one service on this date. ☐

   Total number of children (aged 14 and under) present in services who may or may not also attend Sunday School, Bible Class, Children's Liturgy etc. ☐

   Total number of children (aged 14 and under) who **only** attend Sunday School, Bible Class, Children's Liturgy etc on a Sunday but are **not** present in Sunday services. ☐

   If no service was held here on 11/12 May, please insert the frequency with which worship services are held here. ☐

AGE & GENDER

6. We appreciate that it is difficult, but it would be a great help if you could please estimate the approximate numbers by sex and age group of those attending this church on 11/12 May 2002 (or if your church had no service on that day, the previous Sunday on which services were held).

	Children aged 11 and under	Young people aged 12-14	Teenagers aged 15-19	Young adults aged 20-29	Adults aged 30-44	Adults aged 45-64	Older people aged 65 and over
Male							
Female							

CONGREGATIONAL ETHOS

7. Which of these terms, or which combination of them, would best describe your congregation? Please tick no more than three.

Reformed ☐	Catholic ☐	Broad ☐	Charismatic ☐
Evangelical ☐	High Church ☐	Liberal ☐	Low Church ☐
Radical ☐	Other ☐	Please specify _____	

P.T.O.

FREQUENCY

8. We appreciate that it is difficult, but it would be a great help if you could estimate the approximate numbers of your adult congregation who attend Saturday/Sunday services on a weekly, fortnightly or monthly basis.

Twice on a Sunday _____ Weekly _____ Fortnightly _____ Monthly _____ Less frequently _____

Are these figures estimated? ☐ or counted? ☐ (tick one only)   Visitor's attendance _____

9. How many additional people come less regularly to Saturday/Sunday services?

Quarterly _____ Twice a year _____ Once a year _____

MID-WEEK

10. Do you have regular mid-week worship (eg services, cell groups, etc.)? YES ☐ NO ☐

If YES, day(s) on which held? _____ Time? _____

Roughly how many attend during an average week? _____

Numbers in each age group: Male   Under 20 _____ 20-44 _____ 45-64 _____ 65 & over _____

Female Under 20 _____ 20-44 _____ 45-64 _____ 65 & over _____

Roughly how many attend during an average week? _____

11. Do you have a regular youth activity during the week (Boys Brigade, Youth Club, Brownies etc)? YES/NO

If YES, day(s) on which held? _____ Time? _____

Roughly how many attend during an average week? _____

Numbers in each age group: Male   11 & under _____ 12-14 _____ 15-19 _____ 20 or over _____

Female 11 & under _____ 12-14 _____ 15-19 _____ 20 or over _____

Roughly what percentage of these attend Sunday services? _____

12. Please could you estimate how many people usually attend mid-week church-run activities (Drop in Centres, Mother & Toddlers, Lunch Clubs etc), but **do not** regularly attend worship services at any church.

(Please exclude outside organisations who may hire or make use of your church premises.)

Number of adults (aged 15 and above)   Men _____ Women _____

Number of children (aged 14 and under)   Boys _____ Girls _____

OTHER

13. How many of the congregation are involved with community service/care/welfare groups? _____

14. Has the financial giving by your congregation in the past year (please tick one only)?

Increased ☐   Remained static ☐   Decreased ☐

15. By 2010 do you expect your church to have (please tick one only)?

Grown significantly ☐   Grown a little ☐   Remained static ☐   Declined ☐   Closed ☐

16. Has your church ever undertaken an Alpha or Emmaus programme? YES ☐ NO ☐

If yes give details:

	Tick if taken part	Number of time held	Over how many years?	Approximate total attenders
Alpha				
Emmaus				

17a. Protestant Churches

Does your church have Elders/Stewards/Deacons etc.? YES ☐ NO ☐ If YES, Total _____

Numbers in each age group: Under 35 _____ 35-44 _____ 45-54 _____ 55-64 _____ 65-74 _____ 75 or over _____

17b. Catholic Churches

How many people participate in Lay Ministries? Total _____

Numbers in each age group: Under 35 _____ 35-44 _____ 45-54 _____ 55-64 _____ 65-74 _____ 75 or over _____

DETAILS

Name of respondent (IN CAPITALS PLEASE) _____

Telephone No (in case of queries) _____ Date _____ 2002

Thank you very much for your help. Please return the form in the reply paid envelope to:

Scottish Church Census, FREEPOST SCO7325, Dunblane FK15 0BR.

(Telephone: 020 8294 1989 Fax: 020 8294 0014)

From time to time we make our mailing list available to other charities and companies offering services relevant to church work today. Should you not wish your address to be released, please tick the box. ☐

© CRA

About Christian Research

Christian Research began in 1993, but continued the aims of its predecessor MARC Europe which began ten years earlier in April 1983. Christian Research is an independent registered charity (Number 101 7701) and a company limited by guarantee (Number 279 2246). It is committed to:

- Collecting data about church and Christian agencies
- Interpreting the results and suggesting actions so that the Kingdom of God may grow
- Publishing resource volumes every two years such as *Religious Trends* and the *UK Christian Handbook* (www.ukchristianhandbook.org.uk)

We serve all sections of the church in the Trinitarian group – Anglicans, Roman Catholics, Orthodox, Methodists, Baptists, United Reformed, and many smaller denominations. We do not do research for non-Trinitarian churches such as the Jehovah's Witnesses or Mormons.

We are particularly well known for our large scale surveys of Church Attendance in the various countries of the United Kingdom, the most recent of which (before the 2002 Scottish Church Census) was the English Church Attendance Survey undertaken in 1998 whose results were published in the book *The Tide is Running Out*. Full details of our work may be seen on our website, which is www.christian-research.org.uk.

Other recent publications include:

- *Reaching and Keeping Tweenagers,* Peter Brierley, January 2003 (with workbook)

- *Religious Trends* No 4, 2003/2004 edition, June 2003
- *Coming up Trumps: building vision, thinking strategically and playing to win* (forthcoming)
- *101 statistics that every church leader should know,* April 2002
- *Training Leaders to Think Strategically,* Major-General Richard Dannant, April 2002
- *Twelve Things about Society which impact the Church,* February 2001
- *Twelve Ideas to help 'turn the tide',* March 2001
- *Eve's Glue,* October 2001, Heather Wraight, co-published with Paternoster Lifestyle, Carlisle
- *UK Christian Handbook,* 2002/2003 edition, November 2001
- *Religious Trends* No 3, 2002/2003 edition, November 2001

Christian Research has a Board of ten people. Its current chair is Michael Smith, Managing Director of Lewis Springs, Birmingham. Christian Research has a staff of five people, and was started, and is currently headed by Dr Peter Brierley, its Executive Director, a statistician with 36 years' experience working on Christian evaluation, research and publishing. Heather Wraight, who worked in communication for over 20 years, joined him in 1994 and is now Deputy Director.

For more information either visit our website as given above, write to Christian Research, Vision Building, 4 Footscray Road, Eltham, London SE9 2TZ, phone 020 8294 1989, fax 020 8294 0014, or email admin@christian-research.org.uk

Index

If a number has "n" after it this refers to the footnote or footnotes on that page. Thus "119n3" means Footnote 3 on Page 119.

For further information about the Scottish Church Census 2002, consult Religious Trends No 4, 2003/2004. It gives the following:

- 26 Tables of Church attendance 1984, 1990, 1994 and 2002 by Council or group of Councils by Denomination
- 26 Tables of Church attendance 1994 and 2002 by Council or group of Councils by Churchmanship
- 26 Tables of Church attendance 1994 and 2002 by Council or group of Councils by Environment
- 26 Tables of the proportions of churchgoers 1984, 1994 and 2002 by Council or group of Councils by Age-group and Gender with Population proportions for comparison
- Financial giving 2002 by Council
- Expectations of growth or decline by 2010 by Council
- 7 Tables of Church attendance 1994 and 2002 for each Denominational group by Churchmanship, Environment and Age/Gender, together with size of church, frequency of attendance, financial giving and expectations of change by 2010
- 35 full colour maps by denomination, showing strength in each Council and change 1984 to 2002
- 24 full colour maps by churchmanship, showing strength in each Council and change 1984 to 2002
- 17 full colour diagrams by age of churchgoers by denomination, churchmanship and gender
- 4 full colour charts showing church attendance by environment, and page of special analysis
- Page of special analysis of congregational growth and decline
- Page of special analysis of impact of Alpha and Emmaus courses
- Page listing percentages belonging to every religion in Scotland by Council (from 2001 Census).

Plus a HUGE amount of extra detail, in maps, charts and commentary to ensure you get the very most from this important exercise!

Available from the publishers: Christian Research, Vision Building, 4 Footscray Road, Eltham, London SE9 2TZ, phone 020 8294 1989, fax 020 8294 0014, or from their website www.christian-research.org.uk